A Case for the Balkanization of Practically Everyone

. . . the new nationalism

MICHAEL ZWERIN

Wildwood House London

First published 1976

© 1976 by Michael Zwerin

Wildwood House Ltd, 29 King Street, London WC2

ISBN 0 7045 0173 2

The author and publishers gratefully acknowledge permission to reproduce extracts from copyright material on the following pages:
pp.14-15, from *The Sovereign State of I.T.T.,* Anthony Sampson (Hodder & Stoughton, London, 1973)
pp.19–20, from *Le Pouvoir Régional,* Jean-Jacques Servan-Schreiber (Grasset, Paris, 1971)
p.66, from *Planet*
p.73, from *Collected Poems, 1909–62,* T. S. Eliot (Faber & Faber, London)
p.78, from *The Destiny of Europe's Gypsies,* Kenrick and Puxon (Heinemann, London, 1972)
p.114, from *Homage to Catalonia,* George Orwell (Secker & Warburg, London, 1938), reproduced by permission of Mrs Sonia Brownell Orwell and Secker & Warburg
pp.123, 139–40, from *Under the Volcano,* Malcolm Lowry (Jonathan Cape, London, 1967), reproduced by permission of the Executors of the Malcolm Lowry Estate
pp. 154-74, from 'The Burgos Trials', Jean-Paul Sartre, reproduced by permission of Jean-Paul Sartre and *Planet*
pp. 175-81, Scottish Nationalist Manifesto, reproduced by permission of the Scottish National Party

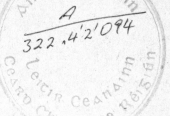

Printed and bound in Great Britain by
REDWOOD BURN LIMITED
Trowbridge & Esher

A Case for the
Balkanization of Practically Everyone

To Martine

About the Author

MICHAEL ZWERIN was born in New York City. He was educated at the New York High School of Music and Art and the University of Miami, Florida. He has been a jazz musician (playing with Miles Davis, Claude Thornhill, Maynard Ferguson and Earl "Fatha" Hines), a business man (was president of his family's fabricating business, Capitol Steel Corporation 1960–1965), a jazz cutie (for *Village Voice* 1965–68), European editor of *Village Voice* 1969–72, has written articles (for *Playboy, Esquire, Mademoiselle, Holiday, Rolling Stone, Down Beat* and *New Republic*) a book (*Silent Sound of Needles* 1969) and jazz recording artist and producer and arranger (Jazz Versions of the Berlin Theatre Songs of Kurt Weill).

He is father of three children by his previous marriage. He now lives in France.

Contents

I love small nations
I love small numbers
The world will be saved
By the few.
                    André Gide

One
Qu'es Aquo?[1]

'When you lay a real liberal against a real conservative
there's not enough difference to put in your hat.' – Barry
Goldwater

A Fourth World folk tale.
High in Occitania, southern French colonies, a lone hippy
lives in a hard, windy land of bare light-bulbs and empty
villages. The road climbs, narrows, steepens. The valley
becomes more worn as the cultivated south gives way to
brown mountain poverty. Tumbling walls along dirt tracks
above Notre Dame de la Rovière. Higher, a stark bundle of
nine buildings, blackened by old fires, ruins rather than
houses. The hippy fondles his shotgun.

The last shepherd died in Venthillac twenty years ago and
the place was left to the bats until a Swiss lady 'discovered' it
in 1965, buying the whole village for $12,000. She sold pieces
individually to the sort who take to vacationing like cavemen
until they can afford renovation. For ten months a year,
Venthillac is still left to the bats except for the hippy who
wants to sink roots herding sheep. His is the only ruin you
might call a house. Parisian heads crashing free in return for
helping him build it had instead copped-out, stoned,
multiplying, ripping him off, and now he points the shotgun
out the window down the hill. 'This is to keep the hippies
away,' he says, squeezing the trigger. 'Pow pow.'

Occitania is not a country from some Marx Brothers movie,
though there are those who laugh at it. One million or so
people – mostly old mountain people – still speak Occitan, but
the number is less every day and it has become something to
discourage the children from speaking.

When Occitans speak French they speak it with 'the
accent' (*feingh* for *faim* for example), which does not help them

become bank presidents or Cabinet ministers. Like Cockney or Brooklynese, the accent is a liability, though in this case it is not a native accent but rather the sound of people with another native tongue, like Welsh English or Basque Spanish. The Occitans no longer realize they speak with a foreign accent. They think they speak funny French.

The troubadours were Occitan. They sang their sophisticated poetry in the courts of Avignon and Toulouse, influencing Petrarch, Dante, the Minnesingers and Ezra Pound. Culture was high in Occitania while Frenchmen were still living under rocks. But the Occitans were heretics, Albigensians, and in the thirteenth century the Albigensian Crusade decimated Occitania. It never recovered.

The fabric of Occitan life is threadbare, maybe beyond repair, so much so that most Occitans think they live in the South of France. Like coalminers in Wales, steelworkers in Bilbao, intellectuals in Barcelona, fishermen in Finnmark and farmers in Tennessee, they resent aliens from the capital. They call them 'ils'. Them.

The old Republican farmer stands on his hill with a shotgun, blocking the bulldozers: 'Hell no! You ain't puttin' no high tension poles on *my* land.' He points the shotgun at the engineer from Memphis . . .

An unlikely mixture of locals from around the airport block access routes to Heathrow. They are accused of being anarchists. 'Lovely,' says their tweedy leader. 'What alternative is there? I've had it being bounced out of bed at 3 a.m. by low-flying aircraft. The entire village has had it. Parliament is useless. All politicians are useless. Local councils are nudniks. The airline operators act as though they are above the law. It's a bloody farce, our priorities are so wrong in this world. Now they are planning a thirty-million-pound extension to develop Heathrow to saturation point. We're saturated already.'

A delegation of Corsican farmers invade the Department of Agriculture in Ajaccio. They grab the director, take off his pants, put a sack over his head and lead him into the courtyard to be photographed by the press. It is the only way they have found to publicize their plight. Until now they have trudged in and out of offices peacefully with petitions. Now they are arrested. Three days later two thousand people demonstrate in the streets. The French occupation forces charge with tear gas, which soon covers the entire quarter. A delegation calls on the governor of the colony of Corsica. Its leader says: 'Mr Governor, I cannot express myself well in French because my native language is Corsican, but if you do not release our friends, we will be down on the streets with guns.'

What turns ordinary people into revolutionaries, radicals into nationalists, hippies into locals and locals into anarchists? Occupation.

Occupation is the imposition of rule by aliens. The Germans occupied France. North American Indians are occupied, South African Blacks, Australian Aboriginals. The Gypsies are occupied. Palestinian Arabs are occupied. The Kurds are occupied. The Crimean Tatars are occupied. The list could go on for pages. Basque, Breton, Catalan, Lapp and Welsh nations are occupied. Occitania is occupied . . .

One hundred and three Occitan sheep-farmers on the Larzac Plateau have been resisting occupation for four years. Today the plateau is filling up for the big demonstration of the summer. Cars filing past dusty hand-printed signs like PARKING and CAMPING. The papers say to expect 100,000 here today. There are signs all over Occitania: 'TOUS AU LARZAC' (Everybody to Larzac). It is windy, the wind is cold for August. The sky moves fast over stone villages huddled against rocks. The bare hills are covered with small, hard sheep turds. Stewards direct traffic. Signs say 'Drinking Water' over clean tanks. Hole-in-the-ground toilets with fibre-board shelters around them. An amphitheatre, Gaudiesque natural rock piles resembling human constructions, with longhairs working over the sound system on a hay-bale stage. People picnic, lie about, wander. Eager-faced students man stands offering pamphlets with pop playing. A young girl with a tape recorder interviews somebody, I guess for her term paper. The interviewee is hidden behind facial hair: 'I got out of Paris after May '68. I was tired of getting beaten up by the cops. There didn't seem to be any hope for politics and I thought I had better find another way to live. There didn't seem to be any hope for politics, the fascist pigs just get stronger all the time. But now with Larzac . . . '

Larzac is a classic illustration of internal colonialism and of the resulting rise of what has been called the New Nationalism.

Nations should not be confused with States. A nation is an organic social and economic unit with common territory, history and language. A collection of cousins. States have been superimposed over nations. State boundaries often divide nations: Basque, Lapp and Mohawk nations, for example. States are often comprised of more than one nation: Alsace, Corsica, Brittany and Occitania in France.

The pendulum which for centuries has been swinging towards larger political groupings is swinging back and just as exterior colonies broke away from empires to form the Third World, so internal colonies – the Fourth World – are now trying to break away from States.

The summer of 1968 marked the end of a certain sort of hope. The left grew tired of attacking the State at its strongest point. The left began to look in other places . . . outwards towards the environment and inwards towards sexual politics and religion. The revolutionary focus in America turned from city Blacks to Reservation Indians . . . from city to country, capital to province. In Britain, Scottish and Welsh nationalism began to gather strength. Autonomist movements sprang up in many corners of France. The ecology movement grew viable after the summer of '68, as liberals focused on the virtues of country rather than city. Provincial youth began to say for the first time since the Industrial Revolution: 'We don't want your cities. They are uninhabitable.' Ecological consciousness plus political defeat sent city youth out of the cities, a reverse migration towards the Fourth World, on the fringe of the system. From London to Wales, New York to New Mexico, Paris to Occitania. City underground made contact with ethnic underground, they were nourished by the same enemy. The State. Not any particular brand of State. *The* State.

Not necessarily together but at least from the same perspective, they watched the bloody farce become bloodier.

They saw the faces meld, philosophies overlap, watched State leaders change while the machinery and machinations remained. They could see more clearly than ever that a change of State leaders merely means a change of passengers in the same limousines . . .

The limousines slide effortlessly along the road, which is getting steeper. The curves are extremely sharp now. They switch into low automatically and straighten out the curves by crossing the centre line at will. God help anybody coming down the other way.

Here come Kissinger and Chou in a bulletproof Cadillac, toasting each other's generals from the bar in the back seat. Just behind them, Wilson and Kosygin in an air-conditioned Rolls. Bringing up the rear, Giscard d'Estaing and the Prince of Spain in a black Citroen DS. They are on their way to the Summit. Other Fat Cats will be there too . . . I.B.M., I.C.I., C.G.E., I.T.T., B.P. . . . initial capital and its machinations.

Meeting the other Fat Cats is helpful, it is always helpful to exchange views. Makes it less lonely at the top. The limousines arrive at a traffic light.

We all agree that a traffic light represents the general good of the crossing. It also represents the individual good. As drivers, we willingly relinquish our sovereignty to that light. But the light has been red for five minutes . . . ten . . . twenty now, and we begin to suspect that the light is stuck. It no longer represents any sort of good. We begin to feel foolish.

We wave at each other, making believe it is just a long light.

The locals have tried to get the light fixed, but nobody over at traffic-light control centre pays any attention to them. The locals have become resigned to taking bumpy back roads. Maybe it's not just a long light.

IN LARZAC THEY ARE PREPARING THE ASSASSINATION OF THE IRISH PEOPLE

A sign stapled to a booth named REVOLUTION. A small, dark farmer stands in front of it surrounded by an expanding group of leftists. He is holding on to a brief-case bulging with lunch. The corner of a beret hangs out of his Sunday-suit

5

pocket. His cheeks are red from wine and exposure to windy mountain air: 'In the beginning we were only defending our right to make a living. We had not yet discovered the political dimension of the problem . . .' The French Army has had a small camp on the plateau since the turn of the century. They rent their camp for a season to the English Army. The French Army needs more room for itself and its friends. A lot more room. Plenty of room on the plateau. Nobody there anyhow but a few hundred hicks.

'The Larzac Plateau is not dying. Young people do not leave. One proprietor in four is under forty. The country pleases them. They know its value in a world overrun by industrial pollution. All one hundred and three of us got together and decided we wouldn't sell at any price . . .'

The mayor of the strategic town of La Cavalerie helped the army in its attempt to evict the farmers. He was its civilian quartermaster. Somebody dumped a load of sheep shit on the mayor's front lawn. Petitions were sent, delegations formed, press conferences were held. Neighbouring bishops and mayors wrote letters of protest to Paris. An elderly guru by the name of Lanza del Vasto who runs a religious commune nearby went on a hunger strike which attracted national attention and he became unofficial public relations director for the farmers, associating their problem with larger issues such as occupation, pollution and non-violent dissent. There were workshops, more press conferences, concerts. More petitions were signed as the rumour spread that the army was going to build atomic missile silos on the extended camp.

Defence Minister Michel Debré announced the inauguration of expropriation proceedings.

A more universal nerve was touched. It was now a matter of defending private property. Previously wavering proprietors were politicized. Some merchants profiting from the camp were converted. Almost everybody on the plateau speaks with 'the accent' and all of a sudden that seemed important.

It was officially announced: 'If necessary the expropriations will be by force.'

The farmers blocked roads with tractors. They drove a truckload of sheep to the Eiffel Tower and grazed them under it in protest. They planted 103 trees, one for each farmer, as a symbol of 'life, roots and continuance'.

Little Feather and a delegation of North American Indians visited the plateau. A member of the Pit River tribe reacted to the militant atmosphere by saying: "The situation of the Pit River tribe is identical to the people of Larzac and we ought to be part of the same struggle.' Janet Mat Cloud of the Nisqually Tribe said: 'I didn't think that I would find in France people with the same problems as we have, and who want the same things as we do for our children. Our children are not made for factories. Our struggle now is for our children. It is for them that we fight to get our land back, just like the people of Larzac are fighting for their children.'

Two sheep were sacrificed in a friendship rite. They were roasted over a wood fire in the fresh late winter air, turning slowly, the atmosphere strangely reminiscent of a Western camp in cowboy and Indian times. As news of the rite spread, more farmers arrived to see the Indians, to eat the mutton, to laugh and to toast. In the middle of it, an army jeep arrived on its way to the camp. Farmers blocked the road and said it was not welcome. The jeep turned around.

A dedicated lady in her thirties wearing a mini-skirt adjusts her Billie Jean King glasses and asks the farmer if their four-year struggle had changed relationships within the community. '. . . I mean principally with regard to the women.'

The farmer says that the women of Larzac are very happy to be fighting at the sides of their men, and that life has become much easier for them lately because they now all have television and washing-machines.

There is a general groan. We are most of us descended from a more sophisticated centre. We sense consumerism and male chauvinism. The farmer is visibly shaken by the groan. He just meant Larzac is viable, unlike other dying agricultural districts of France. He cannot understand the reaction. He meant they are a cause worth fighting for.

The woman whispers to a friend: 'They've still got a way to go.'

My tent is the third on the hill. The fourth, a few hundred feet away, has an iron cross painted on it. Let me add quickly, it is not a Nazi iron cross. It is an Occitan cross, red on yellow, a symbol dredged from a harmless middle age, but still . . . it has to be called an iron cross.

Most of the cars pulling in have such symbols on them. O.C., Catalan stripes, B.Z.H. (Free Brittany), Gardarem Lo Larzac. There is even one Welsh tartan. How different are these symbols from the stars and stripes on Nixon's lapel? The battle of T-shirts and decals for tops of the pops. A proliferation of hoped-for hits. Wasn't there another movement co-opted by 'Make Love Not War' T-shirts? Do we really need all this advertising? Are these new campaigns in fact any different from the old ones? Any more substantial? Does the new nationalism penetrate any deeper than the decal level? Is it any better than the old nationalism? Who are these people anyway?

Who is this guy pitching his O.C. tent . . . black hair to his wings, stringy moustache, balding already in his twenties, just out of the Sorbonne possibly, surely a veteran of May '68. You find him in every French town, his name is Loulou, Jojo, Jannot . . . all the same guys looking the same sitting in the same radical cafés talking. Talking talking talking. About Marcuse, Sartre and *The* revolution . . . the same conversation and they have all come now to the same place. All of them, all of us, we are all here now, and we say: 'Look how many of us there are. And if there are this many here, imagine how many others there are,' forgetting that *all* of us are here, there are no others. We are the only ones who recognize these symbols. A similar mistake was made at Woodstock. For 98% of the population, the Occitan cross is merely one more – marvellous argot – 'folklorique' design. Occitania does not exist. It is not on the map. There are no ministers for Occitan affairs, no Occitan Tourist Board, no Occitan Post Office. And yet it does exist. There is a movement. The language certainly exists. 'The accent' exists. There will be 100,000 of us here this weekend. The 103 farmers are really resisting the occupation forces. These tents are certainly here ... tents proliferating now on hillsides around the amphitheatre, blue and orange tents with bright plastic fittings, of the latest design. Some cars parked beside them have canoes on the roof. Are we the people this pamphlet means by its title: 'OCCITANIA ... colonized by tourists?'

A voice tests the loudspeakers before beginning: 'Look how many of us there are . . . '

A working-class radical finishes giving instructions to others like him. It is too dark to distinguish his features. I remember only bulging arms under the rolled-up sleeves of a denim workshirt and a smell of armpit: 'We represent the "Paysans Travailleurs" [Farm Workers' Union]. We have organized this event in the name of farm workers who feel they are not represented by the larger unions. We are new, this is one of our first actions . . . '

'But the farmers here are proprietors not workers.'

'Our position is that their farms are their tools. Without these tools, they cannot work. They have the right to work. You can call them capitalists if you like, but since we've been working with them, the farmers have begun visiting factories, they have been to Lip (a watch factory currently occupied by its workers), they have discovered another dimension to their own situation. They will never be the same again. Some of them are only fighting to hold on to their private property, but there are also many others who are now fighting for a lot more.'

9

'How do they get along with all these radicals from Paris?'

'Oh, there is plenty of friction. Not so much with us because we work with our hands just as they do. The students and the farmers have problems relating, but four years ago when all this started it was much worse. Remember, ethnics are in now . . .'

'In contrast to the Old World behaviour of their parents, first generation Americans tried to shed their ethnic identity and join the melting pot. Now, with Americanism under something of a cloud, people are rediscovering their ethnic roots and returning to native dress and behaviour. Buttons proclaim 'Kiss me', 'I'm Polish', 'Hungarian Power' and 'Eskimo Power'. Richard Nixon has boasted of his trace of Irish ancestry, and George Wallace admits he has Jewish in-laws . . .'[2]

History is backwards. 'Progressive' Indians (living like Whites) are reactionary, while the 'traditionals' (going back to the old ways) are progressive. Du Guesclin, centralist hero of France, turns out to be a Breton traitor. English victories become Welsh defeats. The Spanish 'miracle' is a debacle for the Basques. 'Bigger is just not better,' says the Houston executive about the mammoth new Dallas-Fort Worth airport. 'I've been through there once and that's enough. All that delay and confusion between planes. It's a colossal disaster.'

'It's all part of an American imperialist plot,' says a Mexican leftist student. 'A plot to conquer Mexico completely and turn it into another star on the American flag.' He is wearing a black T-shirt emblazoned with the emblem of the Dallas Cowboys.

The North American Indians occupying Wounded Knee appealed to Finland's Lapp community for aid. 'The Lapp nation will do all it can,' replied a spokesman, 'but our own situation is so bad that the possibilities for action are limited.'

What does the Lapp situation have to do with the Indian situation? What do either of them have to do with a Texas executive and a Mexican leftist?

André Malraux asks:

What is this country, where the right is not on the right and the left is not on the left and the middle is no longer in the middle. The left is Mr Mitterrand and the Communists, but we were told some while ago that the Communists are to the right. Then there is the right with Giscard. But Giscard says that he is not with the right but on the left. So what we have is, in fact, an indescribable comedy. At least in the nineteenth century we knew where the reactionaries were and where the left was. No longer.[3]

A colossal disaster. An indescribable comedy.

COALITION, a poem[4]

Libertives, Conserverals,
   Assemble to go forth.
Who will lead the way
   Mr. Heape or Mr. Thorth?

Mirror images, circles, dissolves. People do not know where to turn, they turn towards formerly fringe parties. People want something, need something, they are not sure what. They are no longer dependably committed to any party. The party is over.

The Kurds just fought a war with Iraq. The Iraqis, supported by the socialist Soviet Republic, said the Kurds are an outpost of American imperialism supported by the C.I.A. through the reactionary, capitalist Shah of Iran.

   The Iranians said the Kurds represent progressive nationalism in a valiant struggle against the imperialist socialist Soviets and *their* reactionary outpost, Iraq.

   The Kurds, ducking, said it's all the same to them.

   'That's right,' we used to say, 'and that's left.' It used to be so easy.

The Crimean Tatars are a Muslim minority in Soviet Russia.[5] Their first nationalist party, Milli Firqa, a party of progressive federalists, was formed in 1917. It was disbanded in 1918 by the Bolsheviks who considered it reactionary.

11

Under the reactionary White regime of General Denikin in 1919-20, Milli Firqa fought with the Bolsheviks: progressive again. In November 1920, the re-established progressive Bolsheviks declared Milli Firqa reactionary. Forty thousand reactionary Tatar peasants were deported to Siberia by the progressive Soviets in the early 'thirties, followed by the deportation of their clergy and by a progressive pogrom in 1937. During the war Tatars fought with the reactionary Germans, in order to rid themselves of progressive Soviet occupation. Many fought as the only alternative to fascist concentration camps. After the war they were deported to socialist concentration camps.

Flooded by documents. I have in front of me documents claiming that the People's Republic of China oppresses its Tibetan minority, Yugoslavia its Croatian minority, Ceylon its Tamils. These are all socialist States. Then there are documents of outrage against Spanish occupation of Catalonia, Norwegian occupation of the Lapps, French occupation of Corsica. These are not socialist States. Why then do all these documents resemble each other? No matter what the stamp on the envelope, the documents carry the same message. HELP! WE ARE OCCUPIED!!!

Very confusing. The Croat Liberation Front is right-wing. Catalonian autonomists are anarchists. Why then do their stories read the same? Why did Charles de Gaulle shout 'Vive le Quebec Libre' in 1967? The Quebec Liberation Front was left-wing. De Gaulle was certainly no left-winger. (Or was he? He gave the vote to women, nationalized Renault, took Communists into his government after the war, installed social security, ended the colonial war in Algeria. Very confusing.) Why are all these people on the left and the right saying the same things?

The subject is limitless. We shall have to eliminate. With one exception, we shall stick to Western Europe, to those minorities which can be called 'national', that is, whose homeland has been occupied by States superimposed on them ... indigenous minorities. Even here, we shall be forced to eliminate nations whose histories duplicate others – Scottish, Corsican and Flemish, for example. The important thing, though, is the picture. There has been a new layer painted over the old masterpiece and we must take it back down to the original.

Contemporary events will become increasingly confusing if we continue to try and classify them as left and right. Left and right is fast ceasing to have any meaning. We should try and look with another perspective, the horizontal perspective of big and little.

O.P.E.C., the oil-producing cartel, is a group of States working together – working very well together, thank you – who by left and right criteria ought to be mortal enemies. Iran, Iraq, Libya, Venezuela, Algeria, Indonesia, Saudi Arabia, Nigeria . . . every hue from white to black, from red to green. Catholics, Protestants and Arabs together having only one thing in common and that is being little. The ninety-pound weakling who has been beaten up by the big bully down the block ever since he can remember has finally got himself a gun.

Alexander Solzhenitsyn is called a 'reactionary' by the progressive Soviets and a 'liberal' by the reactionary Americans. He supports the church and the Viet Nam War. Surely he must be reactionary. But Solzhenitsyn fights for the old values, for nationalism, now a progressive fight. Very confusing. It used to be so simple. It still is . . . just turn it on its side. Solzhenitsyn should be viewed as neither right nor left but simply as a little guy who dared fight the big State and seems to have gotten away with it.

How long has it been said: 'All politicians are the same'? That 'radical' George McGovern came down heavily on the Indians occupying Wounded Knee because they were messing around with private property. That does not seem to be such a radical position. Didn't I once see a photograph of Richard Nixon shaking hands with Chairman Mao? Weren't they both smiling?

Of course there are degrees of individual freedom and of social justice and in these areas the left is still preferable to the right, at least I still maintain an instinctive preference in this direction, but how long can this go on? How can we continue to tell the difference? We used to quiver at the term 'Junta'. A military junta takes over, the thin lips and cruel eyes of professional soldiers who are used to having their orders obeyed. Right-wing bastards! But now we find in places like Peru and Portugal that the junta seems to be left-wing. Hooray for the Junta! We are no longer sure who to shout 'Hooray!' for.

Take the French left. François Mitterrand, the socialist, was once in favour of an 'Algerie Française'. All right, we all make mistakes, I am willing to give Mitterrand the benefit of the doubt. If the left came into power the wealth would probably be spread around a little more and there might be more social justice. But individual freedom? Georges Marchais and his French Communists are also on the left, they have a common programme with the socialists. Mr Marchais has warned: 'Those who believe in revolution are just dreamers.' I seem to remember Georges Pompidou saying almost the same thing. Marchais has also come out in support of the French Employers' Federation, one of the most reactionary organizations in France, and against workers' participation in industry. And he is guiding the party towards an alliance with the Gaullists, right-wing bastards if ever there were any.

We can no longer afford to resign ourselves to 'All politicans are the same.' We must think about what that has come to mean, and about possible alternatives. Because there are alternatives. Autonomists, devolutionists, nationalists – whatever one calls them – are by definition not the same. Their platform even calls for the breakdown of 'The Same'. By definition they are not the same. They are the only politicians anywhere near mainstream interested in destroying the power of the State rather than capturing it for themselves. They are forming a resistance to this odious occupation, this sinister monyglot conglomeracy we used to think would be our salvation. World Government. World Government has arrived. We are occupied by it.

Author Anthony Sampson describes the situation, taking the specific example of the relatively new phenomenon of multi-national capital doing business with Soviet Russia:

... These marriages of monoliths are unlikely to be much concerned with individual liberties. Watching the conjunction of a superstate with centralized technology ... it is hard not to have some sense of dread at the unfolding prospects of unified planning systems and controlled markets ... as the report of the [U.S.] Tariff Commission noted in 1973: 'In the largest and most sophisticated multi-national corporations, planning and subsequent monitoring of plan fulfilment have reached a scope and level of detail that, ironically, resemble more than superficially the national planning procedures of Communist countries.' Both sides are preoccupied with the techniques of control and surveillance, which have been so expertly developed in the last decade; the techniques are alarming enough in the West, but in the East they have a much more sinister connotation. Both sides have their self-contained bureaucracies, intolerant of eccentrics and rebels. With the dwindling of ideological disputes, the multi-nationals can look forward to a single global system. They will naturally prefer to place their investments in countries whose governments can ensure their security, and the discipline of the work force ... In this scenario it would not be surprising if, on both sides of the world, a new generation will revolt against large-scale organizations, whether as employees, producers or political influences. For however much they may offer the accoutrements of freedom and the financial means to enjoy it, they demand in return an absolute loyalty to their system ...[6]

Buoux, a lost valley in the Luberon Mountains. Cradled under a palisade, the 'Auberga de Seguina', an Occitan inn not mentioned in Michelin. Climbers climb the palisade. Horses graze. The sun hits the terrace, where trout is being served fresh from the stream in front. Children splash in the primitive swimming pool, sometimes joined by a trout jumping over from the stream. We meet a large, ageing, shaven-headed insurance executive, Occitan scholar and author named Roger Barthe.

'States are artificial assemblages. They have not always existed ...' One of the young waiters working at the auberge wanders over ' ... States have lost their colonies already and it is the Third World consciousness which has given birth now to the Fourth World, to the current renaissance of ethnic feeling . . .'

The waiter lights a green Gauloise and smiles: 'I'm not interested in ethnic movements. My land, my nation . . . it's the entire planet.'

Barthe comes to the Auberga Occitana every year for his holidays. He and the waiter have talked about this before. He smiles with fatherly indulgence: 'At one time these ethnic movements were racist, exclusive, narrow, xenophobic, but this is no longer the case. Now they are radical, as a matter of fact a bit too radical for my taste. They consider themselves citizens of the world, too . . . a federated world in which national minorities will be permitted to preserve their personality.'

'Nationalists, in other words,' the waiter says. 'Nationalists are reactionary. Look at all the wars nationalism has got us into.'

'No, not nationalists in that sense. Now one can be a nationalist without being a racist or a war-monger. These are new nationalists. They are not Maurrasian . . . '

'What is that? I didn't go to college.'

Charles Maurras was the classic, extreme old-style nationalist. A royalist, Maurras thought the nineteenth century began in 1789 and was all downhill. He hated the disorder of low-class democracy. Like all old nationalists, he thought *his* nationalism was the best. 'I see you smoke green Gauloises,' Barthe says to the waiter. 'You must be a foreigner.'

'Foreigner? Where do *you* live may I ask?'

A helpless shrug: 'In Paris.'

'Oh, I thought you were an Occitan. I must have been mistaken. Does Occitania go all the way up to Paris now?'

'Of course. Paris is the largest Occitan city in the world. More Occitans in Paris than Montpellier. Most of them punch tickets on the metro.'

'There's no problem, then. If you want to build an Occitan nation, just make a metro here.' The waiter points around the empty canyon. We all laugh.

Somebody once said that new ideas go through three stages.

The joke, the threat and the obvious. Some new nationalists still straddle the joke and the threat, while the Kurds, for example, in the Middle-East and the Scots in Europe are already obvious. The waiter and some leftists like him consider the new nationalism folklorique at best, a joke at worst. But there are also many who see a neo-Maoist situation, the 'countryside surrounding the cities', revolution in the provinces where the State is weakest, where the citizens feel neglected, occupied, bitter . . . where the State is perhaps over-confident. *Libération*, the French radical paper, is at the forefront of the nationalist struggle. A Corsican autonomist told me: 'In May '68, the students laughed at us. We were excluded from meetings. We were reactionary nationalists. Times have changed. Now it seems we were progressive.'

The concept of left and right arrived with States. The Holy Roman Empire was neither left nor right, it was only big. Big and little comes back into focus.

If States are stuck, they are also stubborn and stronger than ever with a technocratic stranglehold on the centre. They cannot be budged from the centre. Alexis de Tocqueville wrote a century ago:

> Amost all ambitious and capable citizens work without stop to extend central power, because they all hope to run it someday. It would be a waste of time to try and prove to them that extreme centralization could be detrimental to the state, while they centralize for themselves. Among public men in democracies, there are hardly any but those very impartial or very mediocre who want to decentralize power. The first are rare, the second impotent.[7]

But now, all of a sudden, history is running backwards. Empires have broken up and States are being budged by a periphery in renaissance. People seem to have this need for diversity. Diversity is more fun. People seem to have this need for something of their own, something that makes them feel different . . . not superior necessarily, unique. This has come to be revolutionary; contemporary States consider diversity a threat. Oh, folklore is okay, you know, wear funny old hats and string beads for the tourists. But demanding your own traffic-light system is going too far.

The new nationalists for the most part do not seriously expect total independence. They speak of autonomy, of federalism on the Swiss model. They speak of political autonomy, economic autonomy, cultural autonomy, the freedom to speak the language of their choice.

Language is the symbol. Welsh, Breton, Basque, Lapp, Romani (Gypsy) and many North American Indian languages will all be dead by the end of the century unless current trends are reversed. Rich languages, millennia old, dying in our time. An historic event of the first magnitude, a tragedy well on its way to the final act.

You may well ask . . . So what? Let them die. There are too many languages as it is. We need less languages. Let's just all speak English. And then we will all wear Dallas Cowboy T-shirts. Is that what you want?

West of the Larzac Plateau, the road descends into rolling pine-tree country, then grazing land, isolated farms, another little valley at every turn. It is so large, Occitania, so beautiful and so empty. The Alps to the east, the Massif Central to the north, the Pyrenees and the Mediterranean to the south, the Atlantic to the west . . . oceans, mountains, lakes, beaches, empty empty kilometre after kilometre. Not empty like Kansas, not rich and fertile empty, just empty empty, neglected like a lovely old hand-blown vase gathering dust in a seventeenth-century ruin. Such a strategic belt, so varied, so beautiful, so much potential. Why is it so empty?

Interior colonialism is much more subtle than exterior colonialism, which has usually assumed visible racist dimensions. Occitania has given France Pierre Laval and Georges Pompidou, among other of its rulers, although it can be said that in a Fourth World sense they were 'House Occitans', letting their origins be schooled out of them in return for respectability and power. Economically it is also harder to spot. We can see Fos, the huge industrial complex next to Marseille, and ask: 'What colonialism?' It is necessary to look deeper and see who owns Fos. Paris owns Fos. It is necessary to analyse who has the high-paying jobs in

Fos, who runs Fos. Paris runs Fos. The locals get the dregs, they are the wage-slaves, and the most they can hope for is someday to own some sort of service industry. They will be the last hired and the first fired. The people who own Fos do not live nearby and so they are not personally concerned about its ecology.

We can look at the Côte d'Azur and ask: 'What colonialism?' This looks like a rich country . . . very rich. Remember, however, that it is only a tiny strip of Occitania and, again, if we look closely we see that most of it is owned by Paris, Brussels, Amsterdam, and so on. The people who own it take their money out. Basically the story is the same as at Fos, and here the dregs consist of six months a year as chambermaids and waiters, or left-over real-estate profits. So their beautiful coast has been used and ruined and the people who lived there before are wondering what happened to them.

France has been described as 'one city and one desert'. The city owns the desert. Occitania is run by and for the good of Paris, the capital of the most centralized State in Western Europe. Jean-Jacques Servan-Schreiber has been calling for decentralization for a decade. His reforms are based on economic, not national grounds. His concern is profits rather than culture. France is just hopelessly inefficient this way, he says. He writes in *Le Pouvoir Régional*:[8]

Take the word 'mayor'. One does not have to know too much Latin to know that it means 'major', that is an important person, a major person. That is certainly what it means in English and what 'Burgomeister' means in German. But the 'mayor' in France is precisely the opposite of 'major', he is minor . . . France has 38,000 practically helpless municipalities. Their real problems will be dealt with neither by their clerks or their elected politicians. They are controlled by the State-appointed Prefect, the Sub-Prefect, the State's engineers, the State tax collector. Constantly short of money, these communes are forced to beg the State to take responsibility for a growing number of the tasks which, normally, would be their own responsibility, and to progressively abandon their rights. That is the process of

19

colonialization. The State infiltrates progressively everywhere where the local authorities are weak and finally it takes their place . . .

French mayors do not even have the right to use the interest on their own municipal funds. Municipal funds must be turned over to a functionary of the State. The percentage of local budgets as compared with total public expenditures is 50% in Sweden and Denmark, 60% in West Germany but only 16% in France. These figures reveal the French abyss; the colonialization of the French provinces . . .

If an establishment politician like J.J.-S.S. can call the French provinces 'colonialized' we need not be wary of its use by radicals.

The word is used often at the summer University of Occitania in Villeneuve-sur-Lot, two hours west of the Larzac. 'There is an Occitan nation and it is colonialized by French imperialism. Our basic philosophy is that every people should be free to control the events which directly concern them . . . ' Pierre Maclouf, a director of the Parti Nationaliste Occitan (P.N.O.). '. . . We are for an independent, socialist State within the context of a federated Europe. Something on the Swiss model.'

Maclouf, late twenties, intense, compact and trim in an alligator tennis shirt, was raised in Limoges by parents who hid their knowledge of Occitan and did not teach it to their children. (Just as in America, mine did not teach me Russian. That was before ethnics were 'in'.)

Maclouf is now learning it as part of 'my radicalization'. 'There is such a thing as an Occitan nation. It is colonialized by diverse imperialism, that of France, for example, and Spain. We are thus pressed in from both sides, and by the multi-nationals who built industry in Occitania but take the profits out, at the same time bankrupting what little local industry is left. The important thing is for each country to be under the control of the people who live there. That's first. Independence . . . independence in a context of socialist inter-dependence. But independence first, socialism second. The Occitans ought to be able to decide themselves what sort of socialism they want.'

There is something tentative in Maclouf's manner . . . as though he is trying to convince himself as much as me. As though he has discovered something he knows has value but he has discovered it not too long ago and the words echo in unaccustomed space: 'The rebirth of Occitan culture is the medium which transmits a revolutionary message. Occitania is composed of thirty-one French departments. If we can give birth to a real national liberation movement it could end in the destruction of the imperialist French State itself.'

I have a feeling of fantasy, a suspicion that this is a movement in search of a context, some generals in search of divisions, an event in search of a location. This seminar on Occitania is being held in France, in a French high school in a French city. Occitania doesn't exist.

We are four hundred, about half young teachers teaching Occitan in the lycées. One of the reforms after the events of May '68 was the inclusion of minority languages as an elective counting towards a high-school degree. Six thousand elected Occitan in 1973 and teaching it is becoming a career. The rest of us are political militants, exotic-language freaks, scholars, journalists and probably a few plain-clothed police. I only managed to meet one member of the working class and he left fast, saying this scene was nothing but a bunch of French intellectuals jerking off.

Robert Lafont, the movement heavy . . . sleepy-eyed, ironic, shaggy, for ever a jiggling cigarette in his mouth. He teaches history at the University of Montpellier, appears frequently on television, is an habitual star of demonstrations, writes book after book and endless articles about Occitania and is probably 25% of the movement all by himself. He draws a map (overleaf).

Is he kidding? Occitania is the entire southern third of France. Does he really expect France to allow its entire south to be lopped off? And those other corners. Brittany in the west, Alsace in the east. Corsica. Catalonia and the Basque Country. Auto-determination would leave nothing but regurgitated cores of Spain and France. What sort of movements are these? They can't be serious.

He draws the borders of nations with firm, thick lines but

only sketches those of States with dashes. We see the dashes cut through the Basque Country and Catalonia in the south, clip off Italian Occitania in the east, all written with Occitan place names. We see another map of Europe.

Lafont chalks some figures on the blackboard.

127,000 km²	Czechoslovakia
191,000 km²	Occitania
13,868,000	population Czechoslovakia
11,610,000	population Occitania

A real country if ever there was one, he says.

The State of France has only existed for two centuries, though historians such as Michelet write as though it has always existed. In 1224 the Albigensians were invaded by the 'Barbarians' from the north and Paris became the capital of a colonized nation. Occitan was still used in the court of Henry IV, at the Louvre Palace, and Louis XVI sang songs of the troubadours in the Langue d'Oc. Occitan remained the administrative language until in 1539 the decree of Villers Cotterets imposed French and schoolchildren began to receive a 'signal' if they were caught speaking Occitan. They could only pass it on when another child was caught. Last one to hold it at the end of the day was punished. In the middle of the nineteenth century there was an awakening of Occitan consciousness which took the literary form of the Félibrige movement. Frédéric Mistral, its most famous member, was a conservative writer, Catholic, ironically very French in nature. The Félibrige did not deal with economic or cultural oppression; on the contrary, the Félibrige is still today a model for distinguished people who want to hold on to old values and prejudices.

Lafont goes on to speak of interior colonialism, exploitation of the periphery for the benefit of the centre, of the evils of cultural uniformity, of the awakening Occitan consciousness. The feeling of fantasy returns.

The most interesting part about the Occitan movement is that it exists at all. Lafont points out: 'Ten years ago nobody had ever heard of the word Occitan, now everybody in France has heard it.' Which is something like everybody in the States having heard the word Indian without knowing what one was. Occitania never existed, it was never politically united.

Before the Crusades it had only been a series of dukedoms and city-states loosely linked by dialect and heresy. It is too big, too long-lost, too vague. But there is that unarticulated feeling of resentment against 'them'. The resentment certainly exists. The movement is an attempt to politicize the resentment.

Jean-Claude Peyrolle, in suede, a natty scarf flowing just so on the side, sporting a check cap such as you might find on Lenin in the movie of the same name. Bearded, hair pulled across an early balding crown with square-framed tinted glasses below it, Peyrolle is the spokesman for Lutte Occitane. 'What's the difference between Lutte Occitane and the P.N.O.?'

'Lutte Occitane is the largest Occitan party. We publish a magazine with a circulation of 10,000 monthly. The best-known names in the movement belong to Lutte Occitane, including Lafont. The P.N.O. on the other hand is very small and cut off from the mainstream. To arrive at independence they want to construct a national liberation front that would include all classes from the proletariat to the bourgeoisie. They are nationalists first, socialists second. This is dangerous. Nationalism before socialism can easily disintegrate into xenophobia, and the extreme right could then co-opt the movement.

'For us the emergence of Occitan consciousness is one form of class struggle. It is a popular culture, which has been repressed by the French bourgeois culture, by an apparatus controlled by Parisian salons. After May '68, French youth was cut off from the fate of the nation and because of that turned to nihilism and drugs. Now the emergence of Occitan consciousness – as well as Breton, Basque and Corsican consciousness – is giving them new life and direction. What we in Lutte Occitane want to do is re-erect the movement of the 'sixties in a new context. A nationalist context.

'Politically, this part of France is fertile territory because it traditionally votes to the left, a real socialist base exists there already. But we are not separatists. We are European socialists. We will get nowhere with a socialist Occitania unless there is also a socialist France. The P.N.O., on the other hand, is not Marxist. They are intellectuals without a language. And an intellectual without a language is an asshole.'

Cautious of leaders, I find myself nevertheless liking Robert Lafont. The way he walks, leaning forward with a boyish eagerness attractive in a man in his fifties ... driving to the news-stand before breakfast to see if Occitania has made the papers, and one day when it has feeling free enough not to hide feeling good about it.

The French weekly *Le Point* hit the stands with a feature story entitled: 'L'Occitanie, Qu'es Aquo'. French children say: 'Qu'es Aquo? to friends in school, argot for 'What's happening?' They do not know it is Occitan. So die languages.

'This is important for us,' Lafont says. *Le Point* can be compared to *Time* in terms of politics and power. 'There are people who will no longer be able to say that the Occitan movement is a joke.'

The article asks:

The Occitans? Who are they? All those 13,000,000

southerners 'with the accent' which northerners have mocked for so long. Most of them accept the mockery with a smile, but some today have chosen to revolt, an indistinct revolt, sometimes violent, with multiple tendencies under the same banner: that of Occitania. This battle for the recognition of an ethnic minority, of a language and a culture, is not only a game of anachronistic intellectuals. It is also the expression of political and economic discontent in a vast region under the harness of centralization for 800 years, and the harness is irritating them . . .

In Paris, optimists say: 'Bah! Just continue the industrialization of the south, bury the nostalgic folksongs under the roar of bulldozers and people will soon enough stop talking folklore.' But the pessimists who regard the present in historical context are uneasy: 'What if national unity, which we believe indestructible, begins to weaken? Will the French choose to follow that which distinguishes them or that which unites them?' One wonders . . .⁹

See how occupation works. The article defines optimists and pessimists from the occupier's point of view. The occupied, however, would reverse the application of these words. The occupier's optimism is cause for our pessimism and vice versa. Optimist and pessimist are backwards, just the way the occupier teaches history. Occupiers assume their cause for optimism to be universal cause for optimism. The article makes the point that the Occitan movement, while still small, is potentially potent. It should be taken seriously, small compromises made wherever possible. Lafont's reaction to the article in *Le Point* is that it marks the Occitan movement's promotion from a joke to a threat.

However, to keep perspective it should be pointed out that had a bomb fallen on the Villeneuve-sur-Lot lycée during the last week of August 1973, it would have meant the end of that movement.

It very nearly ended then and there at that. The last of our principals and almost the ruin of the show is a grizzled crew-cut man with a hairy grey chest and one eye permanently at half mast named Georges Lapassade. He is barefoot most of the time and his one wild eye gives him a deserved air of unpredictability. Lapassade, who teaches psychology at the University of Vincennes, near Paris, had been to Esalen a year before where he had discovered bio-energetics. Now he is touching everybody in sight, looking them meaningfully in the eye. That same year, meeting Berbers on a trip to Algeria, he had discovered he was Occitan not French. The Algerian Berbers had been oppressed by the French because they were Algerian, and now they are oppressed by the Algerians because they are Berbers. He drew certain parallels, and, inspired by new consciousness, created classes in Occitan and Berber culture at Vincennes.

It starts during one of Maclouf's classes . . . a sociology class, a traditional French-style lecture situation with not enough animation for Lapassade. He gets up to leave, inviting anyone who wants to follow him outside for a bio-energetic session. Maclouf agrees and the class trails behind them.

It is a perfect blue summer day and once outside it just seems . . . well, normal to get undressed. Some dance around in a circle. Three stand touching in the middle. Everybody has something off . . . some women in only brassières and panties, some men with bare chests, some in jockey shorts, Lapassade totally nude . . . first dancing then flattening his large trunk against the soft manicured lawn.

Teenagers from the public pool next door hang on the chain-link fence shouting encouragement. Lafont rushes over with the headmaster of the lycée, who is responsible for its availability as a summer seminar and who has been taking his responsibility seriously. He is a jovial, squat, dark man of forty who has spoken only Occitan from the beginning (except, when introduced to me, to say that his English teacher always told him: 'Your accent is oofoule.'), and, although always with a smile, he has repeated many times that the rules of the lycée must be observed even though we are adults. Now the headmaster is no longer smiling.

Yves Rouquette rushes up behind him. Writer, essayist, teacher and poet whose family have been Occitanists for generations, Rouquette has for the entire session been walking purposefully about the grounds, arms stiffly akimbo like a weight-lifter, not what you might call loose. The headmaster asks Lapassade to get dressed. More students have gathered around now. Some smile, some look worried, about half and half. Lapassade starts to discuss the matter. The teenagers on the other side of the fence hoot. Rouquette clenches and unclenches his fists.

One of Lapassade's students from Vincennes arrives and starts snapping photos. Peyrolle grabs the camera and exposes the film. Somebody in the crowd mutters: 'When you have worked for something all your life, you don't want some silly asshole messing it all up for nothing.'

Rouquette tries to move Lapassade against his will. Lapassade flattens himself against the grass: 'I just want to feel the grass push through my body. There's a lot of energy in grass.'

'If this gets in the papers we're finished. People will talk about everybody jumping around nude at the summer university of Occitania, that it was just a big orgy here.'

Lafont moans: 'Georges, why didn't you just have the good sense to do this in some concealed place?'

'Maybe there is a government agent here who will leak all of this to the press to discredit the movement.'

'What does bio-energetics have to do with the Occitan movement anyhow?'

'How can you liberate anybody else if you have not liberated yourself?'

'This is not Paris. This is Villeneuve-sur-Lot, the provinces. They will not understand this here.'

'Georges, I think you should leave.' Lafont seems ready to cry.

'If Lapassade leaves, I leave too,' Maclouf says to Lafont. Maclouf works with the P.N.O. . . . nationalists first, socialists second . . . the 'right wing' of the movement. And yet when the issue of personal politics arises, the most 'conservative' element is the first to support the most radical. Mirror images, crossed lines, dissolves. Perhaps this is the doubt I sensed in Maclouf. The new nationalism has him in a schizoid bind.

Rouquette finally snaps and grabs Lapassade, half-dressed now, by an arm and Lafont takes the other. They conduct him towards the gate. Maclouf says to me: 'And they call *us*

27

fascists. Now you can see who the real fascists are.'
   Cries of: 'Kick him out, kick him out.'
   Freeze!
   The state of the Occitan movement is such that one person taking off his clothes represented a threat to it.

Two
I Gora Euzkadi[1]

'Present frontiers correspond to the interests of the
dominant classes, not to popular aspirations.' –
Jean-Paul Sartre

If you were to go into a crowded bar in San Sebastian and
shout: 'Long live the Basques,' one of three things would
happen. There would be a fearful silence. You would be
cheered. You would be arrested. But if you were to shout:
'Long live Spain,' the consequence would be sure. You would
be taken to an insane asylum.

The Basque Country does not exist. Instead there are only
four provinces of Spain . . . Guipúzcoa, Vizcaya, Navarra and
Alava, plus one department of France, the Basses-Pyrénées.
There are no ministers for Basque affairs, no Basque postage
stamps, no Basque public-school system, no Basque
Department of Roads. You will not find it on your road map.
And yet it does exist. How is this possible?

Judging from Basque place names, the nation once
stretched from Aquitane to south of the Ebro. Although they
are not mentioned by name, it is assumed that the Basques
were party to Roman treaties.[2] They were never really
Romanized however, nobody has been able to 'ize' them.
They are referred to and split by somebody else's map.

I have spread around me a volume of the *Encyclopaedia
Britannica,* one of the *Encyclopaedia Americana, The Spanish Civil
War* by Hugh Thomas, a well-researched pamphlet entitled
The Basques published by the Minority Rights Group in
London, a pile of Xeroxes of the *Le Monde* Basque file, an
article by Jean-Paul Sartre, several history books of Europe,
plus my own clippings, research and interviews. The total of
all this contains nothing more than a sketchy history of the
Basques, the very sketchiness of which, however, is important

. . . essential to an understanding of these mysterious people.

The Basques number about a million. They have lived since before records began around the western end of the Pyrenees. About 70% live in Spain, the rest in France. Their origin is unknown. They were spread over the entire Iberian Peninsula in prehistoric times, probably descendants of the Ibiri, a pre-Celtic people, but even this is disputed. Eugene Goyenneche (whom we shall meet later), professor of Basque history and literature at the University of Pau, France, says: 'The Ibiri had nothing whatsoever to do with the Basques.'

Traditionally they comprised small republics, ruled by elected officials in accordance with their ancient codes ('Fueros'). They elected their own dukes under the Carlovingians. The autonomous Duchy of Vasconia (Basque Country) defeated Charlemagne in a bloody battle at the Col de Ronceveaux in 778. By the year 1000 the Basques were called the Kingdom of Navarra. The frontier between Navarra and Castile (Spain) was fixed in 1016. In 1179, Navarra lost the western part of the province of Vizcaya. In 1200 the rest of Vizcaya went to Castile. Although Vizcaya retained legislative, executive and judicial powers over its own affairs, there was continuing friction between the liberal traditions of the Basques and Castilian feudalism. Navarra was finally united with Spain in 1516, while the old Basque dynasty exiled itself north of the Pyrenees, in 'France'. In 1589 Henry III of Navarre became Henry IV of France and that was the end of that. Except for a brief bloody seven months of autonomy under the Spanish Republic towards the end of the civil war, the Basques have been occupied ever since.

It can be said that the seriousness of a Fourth World Movement varies in inverse proportion to the number of symbols displayed. In Occitania, where there are plenty of them, the movement is still something of a joke. The Basques are serious.

You can be arrested for flying the Basque flag in Spain, or for just speaking Basque under certain circumstances. People are afraid. People are tortured. People just disappear. There are degrees of occupation. We may speak of the French occupation of Occitania to illustrate economic and cultural oppression, but the Basques are . . . *occupied*.

Dominique Pouchin is a bright young man of the left who came out of journalism school right into *Le Monde,* considered by many the best newspaper in the world. He had been sent to Brittany to write a minor story about the renaissance of the folklore but just then the Breton Liberation Front was banned after a series of explosions and since he was on the scene he interviewed all the experts and became an instant expert himself. Then he was sent to the Basque Country and wrote some stories from there. I read them and called him. He directed me to many people in the Basque Country. He did not direct me to Eugene Goyenneche.

I ask Goyenneche: 'What do you think of the Carrero Blanco affair?'

'Chapeau!' Hats off. The Basque guerilla organization E.T.A. (Euskadi Ta Azkatasuna: 'Basque Homeland and Liberty') had just taken credit for the blowing up of Admiral Louis Carrero Blanco, Premier of Spain, Franco's chosen successor. Goyenneche is not a member of E.T.A. He is a member of the P.N.V. (Parti Nationalista Vasco: 'Basque Nationalist Party'). The former is left, militant, socialist . . . the latter right, moderate, bourgeois, Christian nationalist. Why then does Goyenneche give E.T.A. a 'chapeau!'?

'The concept of the State is finished. Kaput. The State is no longer sovereign, no State is independent any more. So in effect the frontiers of the nineteenth century are dead, meaningless. The armies held over from the nineteenth century are meaningless. Even the old areas of economic interests are dead because if one day Germany should collapse, France would collapse too and vice versa. But to be Basque, that still means something. And it will mean more and more . . .'

Eugene Goyenneche is a short man with a tall face, looking older than his fifty-four years, heavily lined, a John Ford face with a full head of trim grey hair, a quick smile and a professorial air with more than his share of sarcasm. He lives in a large grey stucco house in Ustaritz, 'France', overlooking a shady garden and a bubbling river. His study is at the end of a long, high, cold hall with books floor to ceiling and wall to wall, and piled high on his desk making him look even smaller through them. He chain smokes and chain coughs and

31

looks very tired. He lost a few nights' sleep last week.

Easter week. Traditionally the Basques gather around the sacred oak of Guernica, for centuries a symbol of Basque freedom, on Easter Sunday. Since 1968, however, there has been no such gathering because the various Basque organizations have not wanted to provoke repressive measures. This year the P.N.V. decided to organize a symbolic action. They smuggled their 77-year-old President in Exile Jesus-Maria de Leizaola down from Paris and across the border for the day. The event was covered by *Le Monde*'s new ethnic expert Dominique Pouchin, who wrote that it was a brave but rather sad attempt by the old boys to prove their relevance. The more militant, youthful E.T.A. had just, after all, disrupted the heart of Spain, the succession itself. Pouchin wrote that the action did not make the P.N.V. any more relevant.

'Chapeau. Chapeau to E.T.A. Down there it's war. You must react to violence violently. But our action last week was also important. We showed what nincompoops the Spanish police are for one thing. We smuggled sixty people across the frontier, most of them with false papers, many were armed and we stood around the oak in Guernica for an hour. It was a well-planned and brave action if I do say so myself. Despite what that scared little radical wrote in *Le Monde*. What's his name? Poussin . . . ?'

Poussin means 'newly hatched chick' in French. It took me several repetitions to realize Goyenneche was not calling Pouchin 'Poussin' by mistake.

'Poussin . . . dear little Poussin. Boy, let me tell you that little poussin was scared. He was shaking like a leaf. Maybe we are a bunch of old irrelevant farts, but I'll tell you he sure did look scared.'

He goes on for a long time about how frightened 'Poussin' was . . . looking over his shoulder, asking how soon they would be getting out of there . . . contrasting this with the bravery of the main party and their old president.

I saw that here again was a traditional left-right appearance masking the real matter of big-little. What Goyenneche is implying by his condescending manner towards 'Poussin', is not that he is a coward because he is on the left, but because he is *French*. Otherwise he is giving 'chapeau's all afternoon to the left, to E.T.A., the *Basque* left. The French are sissies, soft, not quite up to the job, out of shape. All French. All Spaniards. 'France' and 'Spain' have only existed for some hundreds of years while the Basques have been around for thousands and will still be around long after you French and Spaniards have perished from your corruption and fear. (It must be said that I do not believe Goyenneche's description of Pouchin in Guernica. Goyenneche is smart enough to use the media against itself.)

'We wanted to prove that the frontier doesn't exist, that it is made of Swiss cheese, and I think we did. We passed down and back without a problem, over sixty people . . . plus one poussin, one little chickadee. Borders are myths. Borders have lost all meaning. The French/Belgian border, for example, borders nothing, controls nothing. French Alsatian workers cross into German Switzerland and Germany itself to work each day by the thousands. French Basques cross into the Spanish Basque Country at will. State frontiers have not been around so long that we should consider them irrevocable. Hitler could have crossed the Swiss frontier any time he wanted to. It wasn't the frontier that kept him out, it was the fact that the German-Swiss were in very good shape, they controlled their own affairs and did not need any outside "help". He knew he would have no support there. The nature of the people kept Hitler out, not the frontier.'

'Can you tell me something about the Basque language?'

'There are theories tying Basque to several Caucasian languages, entire books as a matter of fact, and all sorts of theories of how it came directly from Greek and/or Roman, theory after theory, but the only theory that seems to hold up is that Basque was spoken along both sides of the Pyrenees since before Latin or Greek and has absolutely nothing to do, except through borrowed words and cross-fertilization, with any other language known to man. It makes Basque a difficult language to learn. It makes the Basques difficult to understand. We are different. And we should like to remain different. Who else are you going to interview?'

I read him my list, he generally approves. 'Did Poussin give you those names?'

'Most of them.'

'But he didn't give you mine, did he?'

'No.'

'No, I'll bet he didn't. He was afraid I might upset his gauchiste philosophy. We are supposed to be dead and buried according to that philosophy. He was probably also afraid I would tell you how scared he was in Guernica. Boy, was he shaking, shaking like a little chicken. While all of us old has-beens were running a smooth and courageous operation. Never mind . . .' Goyenneche pours two Pernods. '. . . A toast. Here's to all the little Poussins in Paris . . . and Madrid . . .'

The Industrial Revolution arrived at the end of the nineteenth century. The Basques were shipbuilders by tradition, due largely to the oak forests of Vizcaya. After iron-ore deposits were discovered nearby, Bilbao's steel, shipping and related industries flourished. Banks flourished. Basque banks opened branches throughout Spain. The bourgeoisie built clubs and mansions. Economic power gave birth to renewed nationalism, based selfishly on the reluctance to share riches, a situation not unlike that of Biafra in the 1960s. But based also on a sense of being drained, of paying more in taxes than they received in services, based on centuries of cultural negation, exploitation . . . occupation.

Sabino Aranda formed the P.N.V. in 1885. It was bourgeois, intellectual nationalism of the same type as the Félibrige movement in Occitania a little earlier. The P.N.V. revived the ancient Basque slogan: 'For God and our old laws.'

The old laws – Fueros – were guaranteed the Basques 'for ever' under the Spanish occupation which began in 1516. They included the right to ratify the king's ordinances. If the local councils rejected it, the ordinance was not enforced. The principle of *habeas corpus* was a Fuero. Navarra and Vizcaya each had their own civil laws, Fueros distinct from Spanish law. The Fuero of San Sebastian (1150) was a mercantile code. And so on. In some areas the Fueros called for communal holdings of farmland, with only small parcels privately owned but not inherited, their disposition being voted upon by the commune. In Vizcaya and Guipúzcoa there was at one time no distinction of social class, all Vizcayans and Guipúzcoans were considered 'noble'.

The French Revolution abolished the Fueros of Labourd, Basse-Navarre and Soule (the French Basque provinces) . . . abolished the provinces themselves, which then became one department of France.

Ever since Roman times councils comprised of men over twenty-one met every two years under an oak tree in Guernica, Vizcaya. There the crown currently in control would reaffirm Basque Fueros. When a 'liberal' Spanish government tried to imitate the 'reforms' of Napoleon by reducing the southern Basque Country to four centrally controlled provinces, the Basques fought with the Carlists to defend their Fueros. They lost.

Despite their prosperity from the Industrial Revolution, the Basques wanted their Fueros back. They were polite about it. They were too busy making money. Agitation continued on a polite level until 1931, at which time nationalist leaders were still 'polite' enough to be approached by Franco as possible allies.[3] Nationalist with nationalist, conservative with conservative . . . it made sense. They had the same enemy, the Republican State in this case. Restoration of the Fueros was offered.

But the Republic came through with an offer of autonomy of its own, which, after a vote confirmed the popular will, was delayed as long as possible because of the Republic's mistrust of Basque conservatism and finally became a reality only when their need of Basque troops became too acute. There was finally a Basque government, a left-centre coalition. It lasted seven bloody months.

The Luftwaffe tested saturation bombing of civilians on Guernica. One defeat followed another. The Republic was finished. After the fall of Bilbao, Franco stopped just short of genocide. The language was banned. Teachers were arrested. Torture become commonplace. And Basque mills began to roll steel for Hitler.

In 1947, from exile, the P.N.V. hoped to politicize fellow anti-fascists by starting a general strike, but the peninsula had had enough war and it fizzled out. It has been downhill ever since for the P.N.V. They have not renewed themselves, and they began to have competition.

E.T.A. are initials which carry the same instant connotation of violence as I.R.A. Both organizations are socialist, Marxist to some degree, and both believe in violence as a political weapon. They consider this weapon as valid and necessary as the Maquis did while fighting the Germans. They consider themselves resistance fighters, fighting occupation.

This tough image, plus the Spanish saying: 'Basques can't read so they shoot,' leads to a surprise meeting Alvarez Enparantza Txillardegui, a gentle, friendly, horn-rimmed type who speaks willingly but with apologies: 'I don't want it to seem as though I'm a star or something. Down there on the other side there are guys you never hear about who are in prison, being tortured. I know because I was once there myself . . .'

In 1953, four Bilbao students, among them Enparantza, formed an intellectual organization called 'Ekin', not really aware of what such a nationalist-oriented cultural movement implied. They merged with the P.N.V., which was then still the only active nationalist organization. But they were 'extremists' . . . one was expelled from the P.N.V. for being a Communist. It was not a marriage made in heaven.

Enparantza was arrested and met two militants in jail (one of whom, Echavé, we will meet later). Together they formed E.T.A. Its policy was for direct action towards a socialist Basque State on four fronts: cultural, social, political and military.

We are at a lonely table of a skimpy corner café between hibernating high-rises in Hendaye-Plage. A French resort on the Spanish border, Hendaye-Plage is a colonial tourist town, overcrowded in summer, empty in winter. Empty now in April, spooky as a matter of fact. All the shutters closed, nothing moving on the streets.

Dominique Pouchin talked to him at this very same table last month, says Enparantza. I tell him about Goyenneche.

'Ah well, those old boys of the P.N.V. are a bit touchy about their relevance. That wasn't such a bad caper, though, smuggling old Leizaola across. Chapeau! Anyway, I'm out of it now. I've been out of it since I came across. I can't go back to the other side, I'm wanted by the Spanish police. I'm no leader any more, no activist. Please understand that. Maybe two years from now it will be different, but right now I can't speak for anybody but myself.'

He looks like the quiet engineer he is, a harmless intellectual. I am reminded of a journalist friend of mine who once covered South America for *Newsweek*. For a year every time he passed through Montevideo he found the same 'revolutionary' doctor holding forth in the same café. Talking revolution year after year, talking and talking. My friend finally gave up on the doctor as a source. Until he read in the papers one day that this very same man had just started a guerilla group called the Tupamaros.

Talking in cafés does not imply the end of the line. I suppose that Lenin spent a lot of time talking in French and Swiss cafés. I sense quiet rage under the surface, and just a little bit too much emphasis on private status. This may only be my revolutionary romanticism, but at the same time remember that every day there are items on the bottom of newspaper pages about arrests in the Spanish Basque Country, explosions, cached arms, hunger strikes, accusations of torture; every day some evidence of resistance, and there are many more such events which never reach the press. Somebody somewhere is co-ordinating that. Remembering reading about the streets of Hendaye packed with refugees at the end of the civil war, I look at how quiet they are now and think, as the man by the campfire says just before the surprise attack in the second reel: 'I don't like it, Zeke, it's too quiet.'

When I tell Enparantza about my attempt here to tie together individual examples of national renaissance into an international event, he is quick to respond: 'The current ethnic phenomenon comes directly from our society, which is becoming more and more colourless. Coming out of this intolerable universality is the phenomenon of a search for diversity. On the economic level, even on the capitalistic economic level, there is a new respect for diversity, for decentralization, for small units in which one can decide something and then get it done without mountains of red tape. So small, organic communities have more of a chance than ever. I think that the Marxist idea of a unitary society in a horizontal form is a monumental blunder.'

'Isn't E.T.A. Marxist?'

'Four of us quit E.T.A. at the same time. The main reason for the split was that E.T.A. had been moving towards a Marxist-Leninist position, that is, the class struggle was becoming at least as important as the nationalist struggle. As necessary as it may be for the Basque Country to have a Marxist-Leninist movement, I am no Marxist, so I quit. We tried to make E.T.A. a movement comprising both Marxist and nationalist tendencies, to make it a sort of popular front, like Allende did later in Chile. We wanted a place for the entire left in E.T.A. but the idea was not accepted by the majority. It was splitting the movement wide open. There was also another point of disagreement: E.T.A. decided to adopt a strategy of urban guerilla warfare, and we thought there was not enough general consciousness among the people to support that, we thought it would be suicidal. They had all read Che and wanted to go into the Sierra Madres, so to speak. We tried to push a more realistic socialist-humanist tendency à la Dubcek. But we were outvoted. E.T.A. split into two tendencies.

'The Communist Party was very active throughout. They saw E.T.A. as a good vehicle for their cause in the Basque Country and they infiltrated us. Their theory is that class struggle comes first, the nationalist issue is false and reactionary. Their only solution to the problem of Spanish fascism is the party line and we didn't think so.

'Sartre's declaration just before Burgos surprised a lot of people including me because he took the nationalist position. He said that the Spanish Communist Party was imperialist and reactionary while the Basque nationalists now constituted the real spirit of the left. People had been speaking of colonialism, about the African colonies and Algeria for years of course, but it wasn't until Sartre's statement on Burgos that one began to speak of colonialism within Europe itself.'

In December 1970, world attention focused on the Spanish town of Burgos where sixteen Basque activists, two of them priests, were tried for miscellaneous alleged violent acts including assassination. Six were sentenced to death. The trial was staged and manipulated by the most repressive elements in Franco's government and the idea was to teach the Basques a lesson once and for all. Instead the arrogant abuse of power and flagrant lack of justice and humanity taught the world a lesson about Spain. International pressure and debate within Spain itself eventually forced the State to commute the sentences. Much of the pressure came from philosopher Jean-Paul Sartre, and I quote from his statement in Appendix A because it is a strong and lucid explanation of the new nationalism. (See pages 154–74)

Juan José Echavé owns the Chez Echavé café across the street from the railroad station in St Jean-de-Luz, Upper Navarre, department of Basses-Pyrénées, the French Basque Country. Muscular, with a trim moustache and smooth black hair, Echavé was one of the founders of E.T.A. along with Enparantza, in charge of the military wing and you would want him on your side in a fight. Spain has condemned him to death in absentia.

Inside Chez Echavé is an agreeable little restaurant I had not guessed was there from the rather neglected wooden tables on the terrace. Carved wooden chairs in neat rows, a charming polished beamed ceiling, flower arrangements everywhere. Our host's right eye twitches often: 'My father had eight children in Bilbao. He worked in a factory and ran a little bistro at night. My mother helped him in the bistro. I have eight children myself . . . ' His French is actually half Spanish and almost as bad as mine. Our bad French serves as a sort of bond between us.

'In the beginning we declared ourselves socialists, it seemed the thing to do. We were reading all the required socialist literature but we didn't really understand what we were reading. Some of us became Marxists. I saw my friends become more tied to the Spanish left than to their Basque brothers. That was not our idea at all. We saw our friends become in a certain way anti-Basque on an ideological level, in their identification with the leftist preoccupation to overthrow Franco. But Franco did not create the Basque problem and it will not necessarily be resolved after he dies . . .'

Echavé excuses himself to serve a draught beer and an

expresso, adjusts the contrast on the colour TV over the bar (an old Raquel Welch movie) and comes back: ' . . . During the 'fifties Basque nationalism practically disappeared. Among my friends, for example, only my one brother and I were nationalists. Today you have to say that 90% of Basque youth is nationalist. The repression has made it impossible for them to be anything else. E.T.A. has awakened the people to the real dimension of their problem. It has nothing to do with left or right politics. Even the police chief of Bilbao recently admitted that the Basque problem cannot be resolved by the police. It is deeper than that. Franco has got everybody scared. But his successors will not be so strong. There are too many internal contradictions in Spain, and whatever government follows, right or left, it will still have to deal with the Basque problem unless they give us autonomy. Because let me make this very clear to you . . . I'm not anti-Franco. I'm anti-*Spain*!'

Ah ha! There we have it. On the line. Big and little.

Along with Brittany, the French Basque country is one of the most economically depressed areas of France. They both have even greater alcoholic problems than the rest of France, which means great. You drink in the colonies. Very few of the 300,000 French Basques still speak their language. There is no Movement to speak of. The French Basque organization Enbata ('Ocean Wind') had not been particularly militant but it did have clandestine sympathy if not ties with E.T.A. across the border before the government of Georges Pompidou paid it a compliment it perhaps did not deserve by banning it in February 1974 '. . . for attacking the integrity of State territory . . . '

E.T.A. had discouraged Enbata from provocative action because of the need for safe houses for refugees fleeing across the 'Swiss-cheese' border. Enbata concerned itself with raising cultural consciousness and actions like organizing support for hunger strikes and publishing a weekly newspaper, now also banned.

Koko Abebbery, editor of the banned journal, is in the Hôtel du Château, a family business he now runs, across the street from the police station in Biarritz . . . small, charming, clean, cheap. The day-room is spacious, sunny, filled with stuffed armchairs. Koko is dressed in an American-style button-down check shirt open at the collar. His greying hair is brushed back smartly and his manner is anything but clandestine: ' . . . Anyway it's the season soon and I'll have enough to keep me busy just taking care of the hotel.'

Biarritz was a fishing village before it became Europe's most prestigious watering-place under the patronage of the Empress Eugénie. The streets are wide and white with many arcades. The graceful old casino is inviting. There are grand hotels, tables with cloths and fancy settings on the promenades. The coast it sits on is called the 'Côte Basque' which, aside from some banned nationalists and ageing refugees, is the only thing Basque about it.

'Who have you been to see?'

'Goyenneche . . . '

'Oh, the P.N.V. . . . We approve of what they did with old Leizaola at Guernica. But we've never had great rapport with them. I mean we are cordial and all that, we invite them to our meetings and they come sometimes. They usually declare their position . . . we are in France as guests and we want to be friends with everybody . . . and they leave. But I think they are happy we are here and doing things, they just feel they must protect their legal position as a government in exile, although I don't think that means anything any more. They have arrangements with the other Spanish exile groups: the communists and socialists, et cetera. When they formed their government in '36 there were communists and socialists in it and they wanted to continue that popular front image. Well, you know, that's their trip . . . '

'Who do you mean by "we"?'

'E.T.A. . . . Enbata . . . my generation, the student generation of the 'fifties, when nothing was happening. We found each other and it was a nice surprise. We were concerned with social problems without being Marxist. We didn't even know what that meant at the beginning. Some of us down there became more sophisticated and that led to the split, something like the split in the I.R.A. which resulted in the Official and Provisional wings. The Provisionals are the ones doing the fighting. Our Officials — we call them

Espagnolists – are intellectuals more involved in ideology than action, more with socialism than nationalism. Watch out for that word, though. Ours is an open sort of nationalism without any imperialist connotations. We often speak about this. Very often. Lenin said that there are two kinds of nationalism, the nationalism of imperialist countries and that of oppressed nations. The latter he considered progressive. Anyway, we don't like to use the word much. Here we use "Abertzale" which means something like "progressive patriot" in Basque, somebody who wants to change society. Nationalism is a world like "left" or "right". These are old notions. They don't mean much any more.'

There is nationalism and nationalism. The word nevertheless has bad connotations. It would be preferable to find another for a new nationalism which is not aggressive, which connotates only auto-determination, the right to conduct one's own business in peace. We could use the word 'canton' (district), the basic local unit of the Swiss confederation; since many new nationalists use Switzerland as a model of decentralized structure this would not be inappropriate, but it seems somehow contrived, I prefer something more closely related to the old word, a term more identifiable with the force of a nation. What about 'Nationism'? 'Nationist'.

Enter Julen K. de Madariaga, Nationist. Heavily bearded, professorial, the most influential director of E.T.A. during the Burgos trials, he later sought refuge in France, which considered him too hot and exiled him to Belgium where he has been teaching at a university. Now he is back with the classified page, looking for apartments. Another hothead in the room, another terrorist makes our acquaintance.

Who are these hotheads? They do not seem like hotheads, certainly not like terrorists. They seem like intellectuals . . . mild-mannered, friendly, polemical. Counting the number of angels on the head of a pin. 'One finds these contradictions over and over again in situations like ours . . .' Madariaga is an anti-Stalinist Marxist . . . 'a double contradiction, really. The contradiction involving the State – France and Spain in our case – on the one hand, and the class struggle on the other. This double contradiction is the same for everyone, from the

Kurds to the Occitans. There are people who take a progressive line on one pair of contradictions and a conservative line on the other, and it is very difficult to find people who do not contradict themselves. Now with Sartre's position supporting nationalist causes you begin to see for the first time in Europe people who can be said to be "left" fighting for nationalism. And it is also true, at least in our case, that people who were very nationalist in the traditional sense of the word, on the "right", are finally becoming Marxist, or at any rate progressive.'

Koko Abebbery adds: 'There are new problems that the traditional left does not yet know how to deal with. Women's liberation, sexual liberation, ecology, and so on. These are "new historic blocks", as Garaudy puts it . . .'

'Gramschi said that, not Garaudy,' Madariaga corrects him.

'That's right. Gramschi. In any case these problems have not been dealt with very well by traditional politicians. Vertical notions are in the course of being modified. Events are moving fast and there are people who cannot keep up with them. A guy like Carrillo,[4] for example, one of the leading Communist officials in Western Europe, revealed this problem when he said that the Blacks in America did not enter into the Marxist scheme of things.

'Neither do the Indians,' I add.

'Yes, one wants to − needs to − feel part of a community. You cannot deal with that through dogma. It does not fit easily into standard ideology.'

I mention the André Gide quote which prefaces this book.

> I love small nations
> I love small numbers
> The world will be saved by the few.

Madariaga smiles: 'Gide was right. Me too, I always mistrust large groupings. You just cannot have the same quality of life with two hundred million people. There is a limit, and I think we have reached it.'

'You live in Belgium now . . .?'

'No. I lived there for six years but I'm back here now.

43

Without papers, without anything, but I'm going to stay. My home was burgled . . . they took my passport, my children's documents, my typewriter and my address books. That's all they took. They left the radio and television. Now I'm not making any accusations but you have to admit that it was a fairly intellectual burglar.'

'Was that in Belgium?'

'No. Here. Bayonne, French south-west colonies. And you, madame. Vous êtes Françienne?'

He turns to a Parisian woman in the room, who was becoming somewhat embarrassed about being Parisian. The word 'Françienne' does not exist, it is a combination of 'Française' and 'Parisienne' and it implies that only people from the Ile de France – about 100 kilometres around Paris – have a right to call themselves French.

She is flustered. She finally smiles: 'No, I'm Occitan.'

We all laugh including Madariaga, who says: 'No, no. It's all right. If you are Françienne you are as respectable as the others . . .' Which implies not really so respectable at all. It was said softly enough, in a friendly tone in keeping with the general conversation, but it was *said*. It reads tougher than it sounded, but perhaps it was.

I try to come off the edge of aggression introduced by Madariaga with a fast question: 'Why do the French Basques always vote right, like in Brittany?'

Koko Abebbery answers: 'They want to prove they are as French as anybody. All the medals come from Paris. One wants to be in the good graces of power. That's always the problem with minorities. In Brittany they also have another problem, the problem of dealing with the memory of collaboration with the Germans. The Bretons are going to be marked by that for centuries. The French are overjoyed to have that to throw at the Bretons. Not here. We have always fought fascism. We fought with the Republic against Franco and with De Gaulle against Hitler. But they always find something . . . they call us "separatists", as if that's some kind of dirty word. If we want to separate from you it must be our fault not yours. We only want to be Basque. What the hell do they expect from us?'

As I cross the border it occurs to me that your south is always north of somebody else's north. Stockholm is 'south' for the Lapps. The English go 'south' to Cornwall for the sunny weather, which is too far north for the French. The Ticine (Italian Switzerland) is south for the Swiss, and indeed there are palm trees, sun and year-round flowers around Locarno. But when you cross down into Italy, you are immediately back north, it looks like the Ruhr and the people in Milan go south to the Italian Riviera where transplanted Sicilians consider themselves too far north. South seems to be more a state of the State, a result of artificial borders after which citizens conform their sense of geography. Otherwise, why are there so many palm trees in southern Switzerland and so few in northern Italy? Why is southern France white and clean and very southern as opposed to northern Spain, which is . . .

A shock! The Spanish Basque Country is devastated, scorched, raped . . . cowering in crowded quarters under a blanket of filth. This is not what one expects from such a treasured homeland. The Spanish Basque Country is an ecological disaster.

The four Basque provinces have the highest rate of immigration in the country (along with Catalonia). More than 50% of the working class is non-Basque in origin. The Spanish Government, by encouraging immigration, hopes to dilute what it cannot kill. And so while experts point to Gross National Product and expansion curves, the Basques point to ethnocide and highway robbery.

All of those dumb, dirty louts from southern Spain with no culture, no nation, no nothing: I hear that over and over again in the Basque Country . . . all of those broadbacked numbskulls packing our hillsides with ugly barracks, jamming our roads with belching trucks, pushing us in the street and taking our tables in cafés; throwing their garbage on the street, crowding our schools. While the southerners say, these northerners have lousy weather and don't know how to enjoy life and anyway they are just here for a few years to make a bundle and take it back down where the sun shines and living is easy. It is what the southern Italians say about the northern Italians, what the northern Italians say about the Swiss and the Germans. There is also the same element of racism . . .

45

southerners are darker, not so pure as – in this case – we Basques, and there is not much intermarriage. The Basques are quartered by class and race and the whole is not large enough for all the . . . babies . . .

Babies everywhere, pregnant women pushing two at a time; every woman either pregnant, pushing a baby or escorting a child, or all three. Visit the promenade of San Sebastian some time around sunset if you want a shock. Packed solid like an Oriental suq, like the streets of Bombay with procreating or recently procreated humanity. The main problem in the Basque Country is neither social nor national but ecological.

Occupation has also disrupted the ecology of Wales, Brittany and Lappland, as we shall see. The white man wreaked terminal havoc on the ecology of the North American Indians. As in Occitania, the Basques are a nation being administered by State officials who don't live there. Colonialism is bad ecology.

Basque institutions are run by Castilians, there are no Basques in the government of Generalissimo Franco. There is nobody to say on the part of the Basques: 'Is this for our good?' No ombudsman to lobby for the interests of the Basques. There is no Basque Country. It is a 'taxation without representation' situation and only a question of time until the Boston Tea Party.

Some headlines:

FRANCE TAKES FIRM LINE
WITH BASQUES

Who is France to take a firm line with the Basques? Have we come to take such stuff for granted? Isn't it a bit presumptuous?

BASQUES CROSS THE FRENCH-
SPANISH BORDER

What other than sheer naked power gives the French and the Spanish the right to put their border through the middle of the Basques? Have we come to take such stuff for granted?

SPAIN SEIZES 14 BASQUES IN
TERROR RAIDS

That's a good one. Nice and ambiguous. Whose terror raids? The ensuing article makes it clear enough . . . the Basques are the terrorists, Spain is just maintaining order. In the same way, when Palestinian guerillas kill children, they are terrorists; when the Israeli air force kills children by bombing Lebanese villages, it is maintaining order. Not that the words make any difference, either way the children are dead, but they do illustrate the extent of occupation. (The French Resistance were certainly terrorists as far as the Germans were concerned.) A terrorist can then be defined these days as a patriot without an air force.

The State of Israel occupies the Palestinian nation. I think we can say that without too much argument. We can argue about the nature of the occupation, the need for it, its historical precedents and so on, but the fact of occupation seems to be indisputable. Or at least the fact that the Palestinians consider themselves occupied is indisputable. The Basques are likewise occupied. The fact that Israel is 'socialist' and Spain fascist seems to make no difference, as far as the occupied territories are concerned. Madrid and Jerusalem are both centres taking 'firm lines' with the periphery. When those on the periphery resist, they are 'terrorists'.

In the opinion of some of its more subtle neighbours, Spain has been a little too obvious about it. Makes everybody look bad. Since the Burgos trials, there has been pressure on Spain to lift its level of occupation at least to a minimal common-market standard. The resultant 'softening' has included a token rehabilitation of the Basque language. For example, there are now Basque private schools, ikastolas, where one can elect to send one's children, and recently a church publication called *Arcia* began to publish in Basque. A copy I had seen in St Jean-de-Luz carried a story about the Lapps. The softening involves permitting the Basques to read about the Lapps in Basque.

San Sebastian, the office of *Arcia,* an ascetic office with lay-worker types at a long polished table next door to the church which supports the paper. Delicately, I explain my project. A visitor wearing a tapered double-vented tweed jacket, with a carefully clipped beard, listens more actively

47

than the others and after I finish a short discourse on occupation, he mutters: 'We are the Jews of Spain.'

He seems just at the edge of control. I had been warned people south of the border would not talk, but this man is obviously dying to talk, not in the least interested in being careful. He picks up his fancy attaché case, puts on his new Burberry raincoat and suggests we move to a café. We find an anonymous table. There is no need to ask questions, no time; he talks about how incensed he is over having to pay for his children's education twice . . . once through taxes for State schools, twice for the ikastola. These private schools now tolerated by the government generally limit themselves to language and folklore. The less 'difficult' the school the more government support it receives. Those attempting to teach Basque history are either cut off financially or actually closed. If a teacher should attempt to teach politics from a Basque point of view, he or she is of course arrested. This man is furious: 'Thank God for E.T.A.,' he says, looking over his shoulder. 'Without E.T.A. we wouldn't even have the ikastolas. Before E.T.A. started blowing things up it was even illegal to speak Basque at home. Now we can hear it for . . . about . . . ' He smiles ironically . . . 'two minutes a day on the radio. You know I'm no Communist, but . . . '

He trails off. 'How could they enforce a law not to speak Basque in the home?' I ask.

'They couldn't enforce it. We have a lot of police here, but not that many.'

'More police than in France?'

'Are you kidding?'

'I haven't seen that many . . . '

'When tourists come to Spain they get the wrong idea, a superficial idea. They think how cheap and sunny it is in Spain, how it has even begun to look prosperous lately. But they miss one thing. We are not free here. True, we have a little more money than we used to and we eat better than we used to, but . . . well, money is not enough.'

We shake hands and part without ever learning each other's names.

Unhappiness is tangible. People tread heavily and they look straight ahead. In Bilbao apartment blocks stare at each other across choking treeless streets, peeling brown like old sunburn. Matching people walk in and out of them, reeling under the double-load of fascism and the church. Pressure, repression, oppression, neglect, unhappiness . . .

It is all too depressing. I get out of Bilbao as fast as possible, then drive and see the same choking, styleless claustrophobia everywhere. Through Guernica, that highlight in the memory of horror. Worse, the present. Mussolini-modern provinciality which could benefit from an air raid, although the last one produced it. How many starts are you permitted? This one at any rate is false. Guernica has everything already described about the Spanish Basque Country plus the inescapable atmosphere of a place whose name is as dreaded as Auschwitz and Lidice. It is all too awful and I abandon a short-lived search for the sacred oak in favour of an attempt to breathe friendlier French air as soon as possible.

Somewhere on the road, stuck behind twelve oil lorries . . . in a cloud of diesel smoke I remember something the man from the *Arcia* office had said at the San Sebastian café. It had slipped by at the time and I had not even made a note of it. But thinking back now it becomes the personification of the Spanish Basque Country. Putting both hands around his neck and sticking out his tongue, he croaked: 'We are like this here. We are suffocating here.'

Three
Dim Ysmygu[1]

'Plurality is the condition of human action because we are all the same, that is, human, in such a way that nobody is ever the same as anyone else who ever lived, lives, or will live.' – Hannah Arendt

We have all felt – riding the subway, perhaps, in a crowded elevator, stuck in traffic or just breathing the air – that all of this could not go on for ever. A tickle of suspicion on a busy day. Perhaps it will pass, like a cold. Or is it a more serious ailment that Erich Fromm has diagnosed: 'Unrestrained industrialism, moral torpor and the absence of a shared ethical vision'.

There stopped being any doubt on October 6th, 1973. The start of the Yom Kippur War represented the end of the expansion phase of twentieth-century economics, the transition to the next phase, whatever that may be. The Day of Atonement changed the equations. A culture whose principal ethic was MORE faced the immediate prospect of zero growth and stagflation. A society with a torn fabric suddenly found itself running out of thread.

MORE as an ethic is apparently not viable, at least for the foreseeable future, without cheap oil. Suddenly, to be English, French, Spanish or American seems less viable. The absence of a shared ethical vision can only be tolerable along with at least an illusion of 'progress'. Occupation requires the support of heavy graft.

The Fourth World has been running after MORE just like everybody else, though with less success. But just under the surface there remains at least some shared ethical vision. This vision is fragile and basically limited to a last-ditch stand against what ethnologist Robert Jaulin has called 'ethnocide', the murder of a culture. Survival is a grim purpose, perhaps, but still a purpose. Because MORE, which had masqueraded as purpose for so long, was unmasked on October 6th and it has plenty to atone for.

The age of MORE by-passed Wales. Now will it mean even less? 'How will the energy crisis affect Wales?' I asked E. F. Schumacher.

Former Rhodes scholar and economics adviser to the National Coal Board, Schumacher had just published a book called *Small Is Beautiful . . . economics as though people mattered.*[2] It holds that mankind has worshipped MORE with great success and our difficulties now are a direct product of that success. More success like this will mean only more disaster:

> The gross national product may rise rapidly, as measured by statisticians but not as experienced by actual people, who find themselves oppressed by increasing frustration, alienation, insecurity and so forth. After a while even the gross national product refuses to rise any further, not because of scientific or technological failure but because of a creeping paralysis of non-cooperation, as expressed in various types of escapism on the part, not only of the oppressed and exploited but even of highly privileged groups.

Schumacher is animated by the new equation: 'The energy crisis makes Wales immediately more viable. The high price and scarcity of oil – no matter how temporary – makes coal a much more strategic and viable commodity. The English government will no longer take the chance of closing down coal pits for "efficiency" and thus cutting itself off from irreplaceable energy sources.

'In general, the more complex a system, the less adaptable it is. Take the power failure in New York ten years ago. One small link trips and the whole grid goes. Quite obviously there are limits to the advisability of growth. Although even small units, whether they be companies or countries, have been guilty of causing serious social, economic and ecological erosion – generally as a result of ignorance – this is trifling in comparison with the devastation caused by gigantic groups motivated by greed, envy and lust for power. It is obvious that smaller units will take care of their particular bit of territory with more care than some anonymous corporation or megalomaniac government. I think the energy crisis will tend to make this more obvious to more people.

'"Balkanization" is still considered pejorative, but the United Nations started with some sixty-odd countries and now you have something like 130 so it's a process which has been going on for some time, no matter what certain "experts" may say. It is a matter of spontaneous need in human beings. As civilization becomes more complex, we will *have* to break down into smaller, more responsive units. Besides, if we look at the figures, the most prosperous countries per capita are small ... Switzerland, Sweden, Denmark. Iceland even broke away from Denmark; it has only 250,000 people and it is doing quite well indeed. They may have trouble with fishing rights once in a while but it is the sort of trouble that is manageable, whereas if there is trouble over fishing rights around the island of Sakhalin, for example, between the Russians and the Japanese, well, atom bombs might be flying before long. With today's satanic technology I think the only safeguard is to make the units so small that no one or two of them can destroy the world. The energy crisis will by necessity start people thinking smaller. And that is the only way we can survive.'

'What about the other point of view? There are people who say ...'

'There is only one other point of view. Ignorance.'

It is easy to self-serve with this sort of theory. One can find experts to confirm anything. If I were writing a book advocating greater centralization I would find at least as many experts to cite. More. Most experts are centralizers. Centralization has been Western society's principle for centuries. It is the principle in power. Maybe there have always been romantics looking back at the past with nostalgia, standing in the way of progress. Political decentralization may only lead to one more level of bureaucracy no better than any other for its small size. Encouraging nationalism could encourage the xenophobic, even racist side of human nature. There would certainly seem to be another point of view. I was not at all as sure as Schumacher at the time. The only thing I was sure of was that Nationism is a fact, that it is getting stronger and that instinctively I liked the idea.

On English maps Wales is twelve English counties, thirteen if you include Monmouthshire (which some do and some don't). This central western peninsula of Great Britain, part of the administrative division known as 'England and Wales' is bounded on the north and west by the Irish Sea, on the south by the Bristol Channel and on the east by the counties of Monmouth, Cheshire, Hereford and Shropshire. Water is a national asset. Coal is another. Sheep are a third. Middle and north Wales rolls and dips in empty undulations, its towns sad and used, detritus of the Industrial Revolution. Slag heads and row houses, a few brave flowers choking through the ordures. Lonely valleys and bare hillsides. Defeat everywhere.

Dylan Thomas, Welsh poet famous for his English poetry, wrote to a friend in 1933: 'It's impossible for me to tell you how much I want to get out of it all. Out of the narrowness and the dirtiness, out of the eternal ugliness of the Welsh people. I shall have to get out soon or there will be no end. I am sick. This bloody country is killing me.'

That was before ethnics were 'in', before cities ceased being unqualified lights of culture, before they began to choke in their effluents and numbers, before what we are losing became impossible to ignore. We can imagine Thomas today, writing in Welsh perhaps, certainly examining his Welshness with more care and subtlety. History is running backwards. We search for what we once rejected.

Modern Welsh Nationism began in the early 'sixties with a B.B.C. speech by poet and writer Saunders Lewis entitled 'The Fate of the Language.'[3]

'Let us set about in seriousness and without hesitation to make it impossible for the business of local and central government to continue without using Welsh. Let it be insisted upon that the rate demands should be in Welsh, or in Welsh and English. Let the postmaster general be warned that annual licence fees will not be paid unless they are obtained in Welsh. Let it be insisted upon that every summons to a court shall be in Welsh. This is not a chance policy for individuals here and there. It would demand organizing and moving step by step, giving due warning and a long time for changes. It is a policy for a movement . . .

'Let it be demanded that every election communication and every form relating to every election shall be in Welsh. Let Welsh be raised as the chief administrative issue in every district and county. Perhaps you will say that this can never be done, that not enough Welshmen could be found to agree and organize it as a campaign of importance. Perhaps you are right. All I maintain is that this is the only political matter which it is worth a Welshman's while to trouble himself about today.'

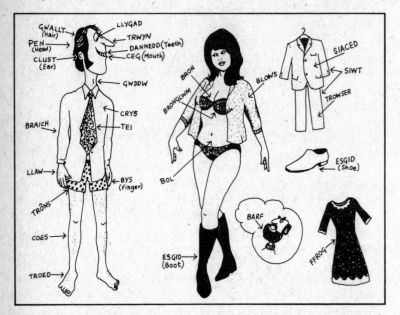

Funny language. Funny languages. Who needs them? Shouldn't we emphasize what we have in common rather than our differences? Gwynfor Evans, President of Plaid Cymru, the Welsh Nationalist Party: 'Language is the main vehicle of civilization. Where the native language goes, you have this diminution of vitality, intellectual and spiritual, and you end up with the rustic, the hick, a yokel chewing a straw. Well, we're not ready for that in Wales. We expect people to be able to read here, to think for themselves and to be articulate.

When the language goes, vitality goes. People become disinterested, confused, drained. That's why the fight is so furious. But it is an uphill fight because our people have suffered so much psychological violence their identity has been almost totally destroyed. Are they Welsh, or are they British? Or are they perhaps English?'

Evans, a gentle, ruddy country-gentleman type in his sixties with long barbered grey sideburns and a soft voice, was one of the three Plaid Cymru candidates elected to Parliament in the elections of October 1974. Evans had been the first and only Welsh Nationalist Member of Parliament until he lost his seat in the general election of 1969. 'Why did you lose your seat?'

'1969 was the year of the investiture of Charles as Prince of Wales. Protesting against another English Prince of Wales, two young Welshmen blew themselves up planting a bomb in a local government office. They were the first modern deaths in the name of Welsh nationalism. It was part of a general atmosphere of excitement and tension. The English Government played up the investiture with a big public relations campaign. They know how the Welsh people love royalty. They lose their heads over royalty. What a marvellous thing . . . a Prince of Wales! We decided to take no position at all because we knew we could only be the losers from this issue. The best thing to do was ignore the whole thing. But the Welsh Language Society decided to oppose and they made a lot of noise . . .' (The Welsh Language Society is young, militant, mostly students who took up Saunders Lewis's challenge.) . . . 'They loved it. I would have loved it at their age too. But it was a silly thing to do, absolutely senseless. It did us a tremendous amount of damage. We were identified with these "extremists" even though our organizations have nothing to do with each other. After the bomb went off there was a terrific backlash. The investiture was a determined piece of political policy by the Labour Party. It was not particularly necessary at that point in time and did not necessarily have to follow that pattern . . . all that pomp and ceremony. At that time Welsh nationalism was going through a period of resurgence and they wanted to re-establish their authority. So, while all of Wales celebrated with bonfires, flags, bands and parades, there we were, the sour ones, the only people in Wales who wouldn't come to the party . . . '

Evans raises lettuce and tomatoes on the gentle, misty hills surrounding his mid-Wales house and he prefers to be called radical rather than liberal. We are in his study, which, like the rest of the house, is comfortable and in good, simple, clean taste. There are history books and folk records, a typewriter, carpets, paintings, piles of letterheads. All in all, typical Welsh nationalism . . . gentleman socialist, bourgeois-radical, religious, reasonable, tidy, nice.

. . . 'Then at the same time there was the Free Wales Army. For years we had been asking the police to take action against these people. They were parading around in uniforms, quite illegally. But the English authorities waited until the investiture to arrange a trial which generated a lot of publicity against Welsh nationalism and timed it to end on the very day of the ceremony . . . '

At the trial, Thomas John Thomas, 21, said he joined the Free Wales Army at the home of its leader, Cayo Evans, who wears his hair long over an earring and likes to ride a white stallion across the moors. 'Why do you want to join?' Cayo Evans asked him.

'Because Wales needs men to fight for her. I love my country and I am prepared to die for it.' The prosecution asked what Mr Thomas had done as a member of the Free Wales Army. 'I cut down apple trees owned by Englishmen. I gave the wrong directions to several English tourists who were lost . . . '

It is easy to laugh. But one should remember that giving wrong directions to English tourists will not provoke great disapproval in Wales.

'Minority' is not only quantitative. There is also a qualitative implication. The word 'minor' implies small, less . . . that a 'major' exists somewhere.

DRIVER SEES RED OVER HIS NEW CAR [4]

Frustrated motorist Phil Bowen was angry when he heard one explanation why the yellow Reliant waiting for him in a Neath car showroom was still unavailable.

Mr. Bowen, who had planned to take delivery of the

car 19 days ago, accepted initial delays because he was
told the gearboxes in all models of the recently released
Super Robin had to be changed.

But when Mr. Bowen understood a Reliant employee
to say that cars sent to Welsh dealers would have to wait
until those in England were made good first, he admits:
'I went up the wall. I phoned Reliant to complain.
Somebody at the firm's headquarters said new gearboxes
were being sent to dealers in England first, and then they
were tackling the cars in Wales, Scotland and Cornwall.'

Last night after gazing wistfully at his long-overdue
car in the showroom, Mr. Bowen, a 39-year-old
machine-tool setter, said: 'Isn't this just typical? As in
everything else, when something is being done for the
benefit of people, we in Wales come last.'

Welsh roads are worse than English roads, its railways have
always been worse. Less people have running water, sanitary
facilities, electricity, telephones. The average wage is always
lower and unemployment is always higher. It is structural,
part of being minor.

During the nineteenth century, if a child was caught
speaking Welsh in school he had to wear the 'Welsh Not', a
piece of wood tied on a string around his neck like the Occitan
'Signal'. It was passed on in the same fashion. Welsh history
was not taught as a subject and when it was finally introduced
it was taught in English.

The Industrial Revolution reached South Wales just in time
to save Welsh. Instead of moving to America like the Irish, the
Welsh moved to the south of their own country and the
number of Welsh speakers actually increased for a while. But
ethnics were out. Assimilation was in.

After World War I some soldiers came back thinking
somewhat less of States. They began to look under their own
feet for alternatives, and Welsh was soon introduced as a
university elective. The first Welsh primary school was
established in Aberystwyth in 1939, teaching all subjects in
Welsh. English was introduced gradually as a second
language and certain advanced subjects were taught in
English. The child became first Welsh speaking, then

bi-lingual. A bonus . . . two linguistic frameworks for the price of one. There are now seven hundred such schools all over Wales. Welsh culture is having a renaissance. Ethnics are in. But it may be all too late, since, renaissance or no renaissance, more than half of the half million Welsh speakers are over forty.

Still, the mood is there, the pulling together of a nation in reaction to economic neglect and cultural oppression, in search of an ethical vision. New values have emerged from the pressures of modern technology, commerce, advertising, the media. It is all so terribly impersonal. And so we search for roots, for identity, for a more humane order. The student riots of the 'sixties were inspired by this sort of feeling. To opt out of the rat race. The rat race destroyed the Welsh; you had to do well 'in the world' out there, an English world, so you abandoned your home and your own, keeping them in the background as a sort of fringe folklore. Now a new sense of importance is being given to the community. In Wales, on the Continent, in the United States. As the mass gets larger, people get lost. People always feel lost in a mass. More lost than ever in a poor mass that is not their own. The world out there is growing poorer. Time to look somewhere else.

Plaid Cymru claims Wales is not poor but rich. Rich in raw materials and with a rich, unexploited coastline. Without its share of the English military burden, a burden Plaid Cymru would lift, Wales would be in the black. They have published piles of pamphlets, articles, papers and thick studies supporting this theory. Colonized Wales has been economically exploited by England for the good of England, exploited for its raw materials and cheap labour. This exploitation may not have been vicious, or even conscious in later years, but it was exploitation nevertheless. No attention was paid to diversifying Welsh industry. English industry was diversified. Wales is only a part of 'England and Wales'. The exploitation of the periphery for the benefit of the centre. Wales supplies England with about half its water. Water has a lot to do with the decision of where to locate industry and yet Wales is under-industrialized because industry is located in England for England's benefit. Many Welsh communities pay as much as seven times the water rate paid by Birmingham, although Birmingham uses Welsh water. Almost every television news bulletin features the three major parties. Plaid Cymru is allowed less than an hour a year. Harlech (Welsh) television treats them better but carries little weight. Only London carries weight.

Because it carries the weight of London, the Kilbrandon report of 1973 has changed the map. A commission – a *Royal* commission – set up by the centre itself recommended devolution of power to local assemblies in Scotland and Wales. The centre can no longer accuse either Welsh or Scottish Nationalists of being 'separatists'. Separatism is now a centralist recommendation. There will be debate and controversy over the degree and nature of autonomy but autonomy is now a central philosophy.

Gwynfor Evans: 'We have defined our objectives by what used to be called Dominion Status. Canada is a dominion. Dominion Status was defined in relation to Canada by the Statute of Westminster in 1931. This is the only status for national freedom within the context of the Empire. We did not choose to opt out, to go for complete independence. We only want enough freedom to be ourselves, to live our own lives in our own way, to take part in international life, to take our place in the Common Market, in the United Nations, as an independent voice in Europe. Kilbrandon won't give us that, but what it might give us is a great deal of control over our own affairs. Kilbrandon has given us new life. Before that, we didn't have another generation. Now we have two at least.'

Aberystwyth, a Victorian sea resort off-season in a rainy country. Waves pound the jetties, the sky is black. Darkness falls at 4.30 p.m. and what with no street lights and little heat, due to the coal strike, and a three-day week, there is more than the usual air of hopelessness on the periphery.

Leopold Kohr, however, who has written: 'The smallest organism needed for achieving the optimum results is also automatically and always the best,' sees nothing but the size. He lives a pedestrian existence from a narrow, attached house on Baker Street, five minutes' walk from seven pubs, three churches, his barber (who also mends umbrellas, although that is of no use to him since he always forgets his somewhere), a fish-and-chip shop, a notary public, a supermarket and three cinemas, and there is even a hill to climb should he feel the desire. Aberystwyth is just perfect. He fits. Kohr attributes his sense of well-being also to the fact that Celtic civilization was born in Austria. He feels Celtic rather than Austrian.

In semi-retirement he teaches three nights a week for the Extra-Mural Department of the University College of Wales, driving to informal adult sessions in remote places like some old-time country doctor (which his father was). One is in a pub in Newport, tonight's in the Rhayadar surgery.

Driving for an advocate of pedestrian existence is bad politics, and besides he is over seventy. It is cold and foggy tonight and it feels like snow; there are mountains to cross, and it would have been a hard drive alone for an old man.

Kohr's eyes belie the pompous name Leopold. They are always sparkling, curious, frank. His eyes are better than his ears, which are in very bad shape indeed.

'This morning I was scared. I could not hear my fingers snap.' We have stopped in an old pub halfway. He orders tomato juice because of the unheard snap.

'Does alcohol affect hearing?' I order apple wine.

'Beg your pardon . . . ?' He extends the amplifier of his hearing device between us. I see isolation threatening an elderly man in a damp clime. An old man who thrives on communication growing deaf. Alone. But remember . . . if he needs anything or anybody it or they are always close by and all he has to do is pick up the phone and call Phil Williams or Ned Thomas or Bobi Jones and they will come right over, or perhaps they will take the time to stop by just-like-that anyway without even the need for a call.

I think of my mother, about Kohr's age, living alone in New York. She too has her friends, but they live in Queens or downtown or New Jersey and they go to concerts and the theatre and they travel a lot and it is unrealistic to count on them. Where time is money and space is at a premium the old tend to be alone. There are advantages to living in a place where the roots show even if they are not your own.

The lecture at the Rhayadar surgery is entitled 'The Evils of Automobilism' and makes the point that the problem today is not so much a population explosion as an explosion of velocity. We all move so fast so far so often that we pass each other many times a day in intertwining circles. We occupy too much space at the same time. We should slow down, move less, retrench.

A fresh-faced elderly woman with a copy of *Portrait of a Lady* on her lap asks: 'Are you suggesting we go back to the Middle Ages?'

'A retreat can be an advance, as with some moves in chess. There are times when it is necessary to go back, to retreat not in defeat but as a gathering of strength. At the edge of a precipice, there is only one way to go . . . back.'

I have visited Wales rather than Ireland because the double-minority problem in Ireland is economic, religious and political. Basically not cultural. The problem does not involve a national homeland occupied by a State. Gaelic is not the basis for a national movement anywhere. On the contrary, the accelerating decline of Gaelic in a free Ireland is the example many Welsh Nationists use to say: 'We prefer a Welsh Wales to a free Wales if such a choice has to be made.' While Scotland may have the most viable Nationist movement in Europe today, it too lacks a cultural base. The issue there is economic, the control of its own natural resources. Wales has that level as well, plus the cultural level – the root level that tends to make occupation intolerable.

Scotland will possibly be the first nation in Europe to receive at least relative autonomy in the twentieth century. Devolution for the most pecuniary of reasons, and I have consequent doubts about its character. But it will come, much as it came to Algeria – not coincidentally after the exploitation of its oil. By now the uselessness of resisting mainstream autonomous sentiment is clearer than it was before the formation of the Third World, and England is at least one notch less centralist and authoritarian than France so it may come peacefully.

A recent manifesto of the Scottish Nationalist Party lays out the economic case for the entire Fourth World and so I reprint it at length in Appendix B. (See pages 175–81). It was issued just prior to the elections of October 10th, 1974, in which the S.N.P. captured eleven seats at Westminster with one third of the popular vote. Only two years earlier they had one seat and were still a joke.

Bobi Jones raises his eyebrows, rubs his palms and leans forward in eagerness: 'Actually, we are fortunate, you know. It is very exciting to be in a small country during an awakening of consciousness . . . ' A thin figure perched on a wooden armchair. Not an armchair for sinking into, one hair shirt of an armchair and the room matches. Nothing too sexy. His shoes sparkle, there are no ashtrays and at seven Sunday evening his wife is in church. He talks at length about the Welsh non-conformist church and its importance to the culture past and present. The decline of religion has led to the decline of the culture, he says . . . and says and says, and I understand why, his Nationism notwithstanding, Jones was chosen to teach the Prince of Wales Welsh before the investiture. This is not my idea of a revolutionary but at the same time remember that one of the revolutionary facets of Nationism is its sometimes bourgeois façade. Church-going intellectuals and clean poets who teach princes are put into revolutionary stances more or less despite themselves. Their reasonable ethnic demands are revolutionary whether they like it or not because they call for the end of the capitalist State as we know it. They are thus as radical as any Maoist. The fact that they do not look, act or speak as traditional left-wing radicals is one of Nationism's strongest assets.

'For us the language is central to the movement. I'm not sure how this works in other places. The Irish are so hard to understand. The Welsh are much simpler. But we are all related to each other. We are very much aware of our links. There is close contact between the Welsh and Scottish nationalists, for example. We attend each other's meetings, and so on. We feel our diversity as a unifying factor, an identifying factor. Perhaps Switzerland feels its canton diversity as a unifying factor in the same way. Every nation has its own contribution to make to the patchwork quilt of international life. The language makes this possible.

'Some people I suppose look on us as being old-fashioned, in-bred, narrow. But, on the contrary, we have no choice but to be international. We can't help it. We have internationalism imposed on us. We are so small we absolutely must depend on the rest of the world, we can have no illusions about it. We eat this with our daily bread. But we also feel ourselves a team. You know, one of the advantages of living in a small community like Wales is that we have to be more creative. We are stretched. If we are going to maintain a living culture we have to work for it. We have to produce everything ourselves. So you will find a school teacher working in the evening to translate Plato into Welsh. There is nobody else to do it. We cannot afford to be lazy, we are forced to fulfil ourselves.'

These are professional ethnics, people whose ethnicity is their main subject of thought and work. This is narrow, though narrowness does not preclude depth. Roots have depth, tenacity in one place. However, narrowness does preclude breadth and, broad if not deep, I am out of my element. I would stagnate in one place. One month off the road and I get itchy. I am a creeper, a crawler trying to cling everywhere at the same time. I am even a threat to roots.

Threat because there is a side of me – or of them, depending – which forces me to be sceptical of roots. For example the story in today's paper about a group of West Virginian miners who are threatening to shut down all the industry in their valley unless $500,000 worth of new 'anti-Christian, anti-American, Communist, filthy language' textbooks are removed from their public schools. The miners ignored pleas from their own union leadership to go back to work. They formed picket lines at two oil refineries and a heavy equipment manufacturing company where a few broken windscreens were reported.

One miner said: 'We don't teach this kind of stuff at home, we don't want it in school. We want them out for good. Right now. Or we ain't goin' nowhere. With these books they'll be atheists by the time they're twelve years old.'

Two of the objectionable passages are:

Most people think that cheating is wrong, even if it is only to get a penny. Do you think there is ever a time when it might be right? Tell when it is. Tell why you think it is right.

It is time to shake up the student council. We need a new constitution granting power to the students. We want real power.

This sort of thing makes one wonder about ethnics, question the principle of devolution itself. It is the dark side of the locals around Heathrow, the Corsican farmers, the events on the Larzac. One can also be rooted in prejudice. States Rights in the United States has always been a euphemism for the legalization of local prejudice. During the civil rights movement, I for one was very much a centralist. I thought the central government had every right and obligation to impose its will on the locals. The difference there was that the locals had no more shared ethical vision than the centre, and they were even less enlightened. Small is not beautiful per se. Small can be pejorative, as in 'a small mind'. But occupation has become much more oppressive, intolerable and inefficient in the ensuing decade. It may be necessary to defend demands for auto-determination unconditionally, no matter how misguided, on the principle that the State is the biggest enemy. The State is *the* enemy and anybody, anybody at all fighting it is to be encouraged. We should perhaps worry about the biggest enemy first and only then about what follows.

Wales, however, is easier. The lines are clearly drawn. There are the occupiers and the occupied. The bad guys and the good guys. Bad not in a vicious sense, just inefficient, old-fashioned, unfair. In Wales the good guys are even easy. There is only one Nationalist party, Plaid Cymru, with right and left wings it is true, but basically only one grouping. Very orderly, tidy, ironically very English. They are socialists and pacifists. Nationalism based on a true nation with organic territory, culture, history and language, built on pacifist socialism is hard to fault.

'Yeah, I'll bet. I'll bet you're a journalist. I know what paper you're with too. The *Police Gazette* . . . '

Dafydd Iwan, square-jawed, blunt-nosed, shaggy-haired, rock-fisted . . . angry. Chairman of the Welsh Language

Society from 1968 to 1971, Iwan now runs a small record company called 'Sian', the office of which we are in. A one-storey brick building in the ruins of what was intended to be an industrial park just outside the northern Welsh town of Pen-y-groes.

'Well, anyway, I get the impression that there are about ten of you people writing books about Wales because I've answered questions like this before. Too many questions . . .'

It is strangely welcome, some aggression in Wales. Not the aggression specifically, just some violent emotion. Everybody in Wales has been so bloody *nice*. You may say that some people are pretty hard to please, but there are times when niceness is not enough. Niceness alone is an absence of spirit, weakness, even a certain kind of condescension. Niceness alone is bland, superficial, respectable. Too much respectability. Too much Bible talk. Too many shined shoes and not enough ashtrays. One has the feeling around Plaid Cymru that to smoke is objectionable not because it is unhealthy but because it is sinful. There are nice people in Westminster too. Nice people can do naughty things. Perhaps this is quibbling but Gwynfor Evans said that Plaid Cymru complained to the police about the Free Wales Army. The Free Wales Army had done nothing to Plaid Cymru, nobody was robbed or mugged. And yet they called the cops . . . English cops, the occupier's cops. 'I say, we have these chaps here running around with earrings. Terribly untidy.' This would not seem such a nice thing to do on occupied territory. I wonder how a Welsh Government would treat its Pakistani minority. Talk of purity can turn easily into master race talk.

John Jenkins was sentenced to ten years on April 20th, 1970, for several water pipe-line explosions. There was not much sympathy for this sort of thing then because the Nationists were being nice after the 'counter-productive' events around the investiture. Now, however, one reads headlines like 'Welsh nationalists want water tax' and it appears that Jenkins was in fact not counter-productive, only ahead of his time. Violence, or the fear of it, is always productive in minority causes. First you have to get their attention.

Excerpts from Jenkins's jail letters were published in the

Welsh magazine, *Planet:*

Mother Wales is not a beautiful young girl after whom I
lust, or an old duchess whose money and status I desire:
she is old, well past her best, decrepit, boozy, and has
taken strange bedfellows without the saving grace of
desperation . . . The fight was not to stop water but to
create a state of mind, the blowing up of the water pipes
was strategy and I am paying heavily. But I will be able
to look my grandchildren in the eyes when they ask the
question: 'and when Wales was being destroyed in the
sixties, where were you?'

I am afraid I am a terrible heretic now in what I am
about to say, but I do not see the light in Plaid Cymru's
tunnel. The party's leaders are possessed by a strange
logic very similar to the English one which believes fully
in independence for everyone except Wales. They send
messages of solidarity to Makarios, questions are asked
in the House about the Basques, they write articles about
the Bretons and the people of Catalonia; but they have
delighted the establishment by refusing to mention me or
what I stood for in their nationalist press, the only hope I
ever had of allowing the people to see my side. Let us
agree that if something does not happen soon the Wales
we know will vanish, the Wales we wish will never be. At
least the only price of my ideals is the loss of my freedom;
the leaders of Plaid Cymru are prepared to accept
the loss of Wales itself as the price of their respectability.
They seem to believe that because what they want is
right and what their opponents want is wrong, that they
will automatically get it. I would suggest they put the
Bible down and study their history books, particularly
the British Empire parts. Even their biblical knowledge
is biased and partisan – had they made rather less of Job,
then I would not have had to make more of David. I
oppose the leaders of Plaid Cymru because they are
prepared to sacrifice their people, their country and their
heritage on the shrine of their respectability and
pacifism.

Raising consciousness is not easy. It always takes an unpopular avant garde ready to risk prison. The people would like to ignore their occupation. The invasion comes slowly and easily, not like an occupation at all, and it is welcome at first. More jobs for the men, more business in the shops. But after a while you see that the place is not the same, your own town no longer belongs to you, there is no space left for you, and the people who have bought and built here don't care about the place because they are only here two months a year if at all. The people who live here have become the minority and can no longer afford the houses or land and the shops close because there are supermarkets in the next town and the people who own the supermarkets and the land take all their capital back to the capital anyway. The place is dying.

Cymdeithas Yr Iaith Gymraeg, The Welsh Language Society, was formed after Saunders Lewis's speech and its young members began going to jail for what were termed 'language offences'. They thought the only way for Welsh culture to survive was through English jails. Their slogan: 'No violence of fist, no violence of word, no violence of heart.' Property, however, was fair game on the principle that what does violence deserves violence.

They destroyed English-only road signs, refused to pay taxes because the forms were only in English, removed automobile tax stamps from windscreens for the same reason, set off explosions to protest the drowning of valleys. These were not hippies, yippies or counter-cultural outlaws. The movement has nothing, or little, to do with drugs. Many still go to church. They were just angry ethnics and after such a straight and respected figure as Saunders Lewis (Bobi Jones calls him the 'greatest living Welshman') called for action, the W.L.S. found many supporters. The policy was to attack one issue at a time, and the issue for the few years before the investiture was the drowning of the valleys.

Welsh water was badly needed for Birmingham and Liverpool, a crash programme of reservoir construction passed. London picked what valleys to flood. Sometimes there were villages at the bottom of them. There was no understandng of the life that goes on in these villages, or there was no caring. They were to be sacrificed in the name of progress. Only a bunch of hicks anyway, like the 103 farmers on the Larzac. It is extraordinary how similar the problems of the Fourth World are, whether the State involved is socialist, capitalist, fascist or communist. Being little is what counts. Minor.

One of those drowned was a valley near Bala, the heart of Welsh Wales. There was a village in it, with a school, a chapel and a few houses. It was a cultured valley, a valley of harpists and poets. (To be a poet means a lot in Wales.) With it were drowned roots centuries old. Plaid Cymru fought it through Westminster and even English M.P.s voted against it but, though this was one issue all of Wales was behind, the majority is still English in Westminster and the majority wins. The Welsh Language Society saw legalities and petitions would come to nothing and it was this feeling of frustration that led to the bomb disaster before the investiture.

The small and cluttered office of the Welsh Language Society above a bookshop in Aberystwyth. A bilingual flyer advertising the latest issue:

WALES IS NOT FOR SALE

In some Welsh villages, between 40% and 50% of the homes are holiday homes.
The demand for holiday homes is rising rapidly, and so are the prices paid for them (£21,000 and £15,000 were paid for two this year).
Local people cannot compete; many cannot afford a home of their own, and many more live in sub-standard houses.
Yet hundreds of thousands of pounds are paid out every year in grants to modernise second homes of wealthy middle-class Englishmen.
This flood of holidaymakers is pricing Welshmen out of a home, erodes the culture of rural Wales, and over-burdens our public services.

WE SAY THAT THE PEOPLE OF WALES SHOULD COME FIRST, AND THAT OUR BIRTHRIGHT SHOULD NOT BE SOLD TO THE HIGHEST BIDDER.

WE CALL UPON THE GOVERNMENT:

1. to stop the sale of a house as a second home if there is a demand for it as a permanent home.
2. to restrict holiday homes to not more than 10% of the total number of homes in any rural district.
3. to give Local Authorities the right to withhold all grants for the improvement of part-time holiday homes, and to charge extra rates for holiday homes.
4. to assist Local Authorities to buy old houses for renovating and letting to local tenants:

WE CALL UPON LOCAL AUTHORITIES:

1. to withhold all grant aid for holiday home improvement.
2. to use grants to improve existing homes, and to buy old houses, modernise them, and to let them to local tenants.

WE ALSO CALL UPON ESTATE AGENTS NOT TO SELL HOUSES AS HOLIDAY HOMES WHILE THERE IS A DEMAND FOR THEM AS PERMANENT HOMES.

FISHING RIGHTS

We oppose the sale of Wales' best fishing waters to wealthy individuals, syndicates and clubs from the cities and from England.
THE WATERS OF WALES, AS WELL AS HER LAND, BELONG TO THE PEOPLE OF WALES, AND EVERY WELSH FISHERMAN SHOULD HAVE THE RIGHT TO FISH IN ANY RIVER OR LAKE IN WALES FOR A REASONABLE LICENCE FEE.

LET'S PUT WALES FIRST!! WELSH LAND, HOMES AND WATERS FOR THE PEOPLE OF WALES!!

Published by Cymdeithas yr Iaith Gymraeg (The Welsh Language Society), 24 Ffordd y Mor, Aberystwyth.

NID YW CYMRU AR WERTH

Mewn rhai o bentrefi Cymru, mae rhwng 40% a 50% o'r tai eisioes yn dai haf, ac felly'n wag am ran helaeth o'r flwyddyn.

Mae'r galw am dai haf yn dal i gynnyddu, a'r pris a delir amdanynt yn dal i godi (talwyd £15,000 a £21,000 am ddau eleni)

Mae Cymry lleol yn methu cystadlu, ac yn methu fforddio cartref o gwbl, a miloedd yn byw mewn tai anaddas.

Eto telir cannoedd a filoedd o bunnau'r flwyddyn mewn grantiau at wella ail-gartrefi i ymwelwyr cyfoethog o Loegr.

Mae'r llif o Saeson i gefn gwlad yn prisio'r Cymry o'u cartrefi, yn peryglu Cymreigrwydd ein broydd, ac yn gosod pwysau gormodol ar ein gwasanaethau cyhoeddus.

DYWEDWN NI Y DYLAI POBL CYMRU DDOD GYNTAF, AC NA DDYLID GWERTHU CYMRU I BOBL YR ARIAN MAWR.

GALWN AR Y LLYWODRAETH:

1. i ddeddfu na ddylid gwerthu unrhyw dŷ fel tŷ haf os galw amdano fel cartref sefydlog.
2. i ddeddfu o hyn ymlaen na ddylai mwy an 10% o gartrefi unrhyw blwyf gwledig fod yn gartrefi gwyliau ac ail-gartrefi.
3. i roi'r hawl i Gynghorau Lleol i wrthod *pob* grant at wella tai haf ac ail gartrefi, ac i godi treth ychwanegol ar dai haf.
4. i roi cymorth i Gynghorau Lleol i brynu tai i'w hadnewyddu ar gyfer trethdalwyr lleol.

GALWN AR GYNGHORAU LLEOL

1. i wrthod rhoi grantiau at wella tai haf.
2. i ddefnyddio'r grantiau i wella cartrefi presennol, ac i brynu hen dai i'w moderneiddio ar gyfer tenantiaid lleol.

A GALWN AR WERTHWYR EIDDO I BEIDIO GWERTHU TAI FEL TAI HAF OS OES GALW AMDANYNT FEL CARTREFI SEFYDLOG.

HAWLIAU PYSGOTA

Gwrthwynebwn y modd y gwerthir afonydd pysgota gorau Cymru i unigolion a chlybiau cyfoethog o Loegr.

MAE DYFROEDD CYMRU, FEL EI THIR, YN PERTHYN I BOBL CYMRU, A DYLAI POB PYSGOTWR O GYMRO GAEL YR HAWL I BYSGOTA MEWN UNRHYW AFON NEU LYN YNG NGHYMRU AM BRIS RHESYMOL.

RHOWN GYMRU GYNTAF!! TAI, TIR A DŴR CYMRU I BOBL CYMRU!!

Cyhoeddwyd gan Gymdeithas yr Iaith Gymraeg, 24 Ffordd y Mor, Aberystwyth. Argraffwyd gan GRAIG 68, Hoel y Bontfaen, Caerdydd.

A quiet, businesslike atmosphere with young people clipping, pasting and laying out, reminiscent of a Midwest college newspaper office. The boys have short hair, the girls long skirts. There is no feeling of rebellion here, only quiet and orderly work. These are not acid-head freaks as they would have been in a similar setup in America, there are no five-papered hash joints being passed around as there would be in similar surroundings in London. These are no wild-eyed Maoists as such an office might contain in Paris. Just nice clean kids your grandparents would have approved of. I am invited to a demonstration on Saturday in the northern port of Pwllheli.

Pwllheli. The town square . . . a bus station on a small grass roundabout. One-thirty in the afternoon. Cold. I have been damp and cold for a week now. The bed and breakfasts are cold. the restaurants, the cinemas, the Welsh do not seem to feel the cold. Raw wind, bone cold, muscle spasms from the cold wind. A gaggle of hirsute students gathers across the roundabout from the 'Conservative Club', suitably anonymous, curtained windows hiding the Old Boys inside.

I feel the lack of a club, no warm place to go, no clan to count on. Friends and family dispersed all over the globe, my roots such as they ever were long withered in Manhattan concrete, at home nowhere, I am everywhere. Do I mistake alienation for freedom? The Conservatives have a club, even the Maoists are a kind of club, the Welsh Language Society is a club. They count on each other. Who can I count on? Where are they? Nobody stays in one place any more where I come from. Everybody is from somewhere else. The Welsh stay put, and if they move they leave their nucleus behind. They can count on that. Roots are narrowing. The deeper they go the taller you grow but transplantation comes hard. Take your pick. To creep or to root.

Shivering in front of a menswear shop called 'Celtic House', I am reminded of a postcard in my collection . . . a colour photo of a dark-skinned man in an embroidered shirt holding a bow and arrow, on the back of which is printed: 'Bobby Tiger wrestles alligators daily at Jimmy Tiger's Indian village on US 41 . . . ' That is what is left of the Seminoles, a regional curiosity like 'Celtic', something to encourage trade, and yet even these exploitations indicate the potential strength of Nationism. They confirm the fact that people need diversity. To escape is an increasing need as THE SAME weighs heavier, and so these remnants assume a symbolic importance no matter how silly or irrelevant they are on the surface. Because just under the surface 'Celtic' means more than menswear and it is surfacing.

However, the clothes in the Celtic Shop are neither Celtic nor English but that monyglot-approved uniform which is THE SAME in New York, San Sebastian, Villeneuve-sur-Lot and Pwllheli. 'We will move soon,' I am informed. 'Just follow the cars.'

The demonstration has been advertised and I estimate at least two plainclothesmen in the crowd, plus the three uniformed bobbies standing to one side. It has, however, not been advertised that the real action will be in Nefyn, ten miles north.

The students go for their cars one by one and we are soon a string of fifteen on a country road. The cops seem to have stayed behind. At least they are not interfering. The cars pull up one behind the other inside Nefyn and we follow the leader through the town to a line of modern, neat, two-storey attached holiday homes, furnished but unoccupied in this off-season. A leader pulls up in a van, jumps down, distributes placards, paint, paint-brushes and putty-knives and hollers instructions over a loudspeaker. The demonstrators paint the windows of the holiday homes black and plug the keyholes with putty. It goes smoothly and fast according to plan. Then some Welsh songs are sung under the placards. That's all . . . no violence, no police. Hopefully, some consciousness raised.

The next day the local paper carries an item about some natives who pitched in to help clean the paint off the windows and unstick the keyholes. They said it was not a nice way to treat guests. A certain Mrs Bethan Cwrwgl was quoted as saying: 'The Welsh Language Society are a bunch of hooligans.'

Four
Kai Jas Ame[1]

'. . . And what there is to conquer . . .
        has already been discovered . . .
Once or twice or several times . . .
There is only the fight to recover
        what has been lost
And found and lost again and again.'
                T. S. Eliot: *Four Quartets*

A minority even minorities consider minor, Gypsies are alien
everywhere. Although not strictly a *national* minority in
Europe – that is, they have no national homeland – they are
however a nation and did arrive before the current system of
States was imposed on them. They are certainly occupied.

Defined as 'Member of a wandering race of Indian origin, a
Romani (Rom) . . .', there are over four million of them in
Europe alone. Legend has it that a Gypsy smithy forged the
nails which crucified Christ . . . worse, *sold* them. There have
been heavy dues to pay. Close to half a million died in Nazi
concentration camps and the measure of their occupation can
be gauged by the fact that the survivors did not feel it was safe
to surface for a body count.

'Hi, Gratton. Missed you on telly last night.' Harry, a short,
dark Gypsy whose age is hidden by soot, greets Gratton
Puxon, warming his hands over a fire. When the B.B.C. wants
footage on the subject, they call Gratton Puxon, one clean
Gypsy. We are joined by three children with dirty faces.
Harry feeds the fire chunks of auto salvage, burning off the
impurities to make commercial scrap.

Gratton smiles and dances to warm his feet, shivering from
the wind despite an overcoat: 'Have you heard? Enoch Powell
came out with an anti-Gypsy statement.'

Harry, although in shirtsleeves, is not shivering. 'Really?
What did he say?'

'He said Gypsies shouldn't expect the same benefits as good tax-paying Englishmen.'

'Cor! I didn't mind when he was goin' on about them Blacks, but I was *born* in this bleedin' country.'

The Gypsy people began leaving India about 1,500 years ago. They prefer to be called Roms, but since the world knows them as Gypsies, and since they often lapse and refer to themselves as Gypsies anyway that is what they will be called here. They moved out in successive waves away from local wars; disunited, vulnerable, small tribes travelling with their animals. Three main tribes reached the West . . . the Roms, or Romanis (which has come to be the generic term for all Gypsies) ended up in Eastern Europe; the Sinti, from Sindustan (now part of Pakistan) in Western Europe, and the Calo ('black' in Sanskrit) in Spain and North Africa. They hold on to a loose body of religious belief based on Hinduism, although practical Gypsies adopt the religion of whatever country they are in. Some are Christian and Moslem at the same time in places where that makes sense. The family – an extended family, more a clan – is holy, and the Gypsy idea of hell on earth is to live in the same house and work for somebody else all their lives. They prefer day labour, sporadic small enterprise in which they can preserve some semblance of freedom, like asphalting, cherry-picking or collecting scrap.

Harry is sifting through a pile of piping and scrap behind the construction site. The Man appears: 'Are you registered?' he asks.

'Have I killed somebody that I should be registered?' Harry asks The Man for his credentials.

The Man has a badge in a brief-case: 'You have to have a licence to collect scrap in this borough. Are you or aren't you registered?'

'Not me. You're not registerin' *me*, old chap.'

The Gypsies reached Greece around the eighth century, Western Europe during the Middle Ages. People there thought they were from Egypt, thus 'Gypsy'. Their roots were on the road, an alien way of life, and anyway there was little

space left for homesteaders. Earlier migrations had already
staked out the territory. The Gypsies were forced to continue
to move, only the fringes of established society were available
to them and their nomadic tendencies were reinforced.
Pariahs for ever on the road, they were often forced to steal,
thus giving birth to the lore of Gypsy thievery. It was also
difficult to take baths and thus cleanliness is not in the Gypsy
tradition. They were expelled ('punishment for Gypsies and
beggars entering this district') and slaughtered ('by taking the
life of a Gypsy the defendant did not act against the policy of
the State'). In 1596 in Yorkshire, 106 Gypsies were
condemned to death at one sitting.

Sometimes they were accepted for their skills –
metal-working, music, horse-handling – in Eastern Europe
particularly, and many villages acquired a token Gypsy
family. It was not as bad in Eastern Europe as in the West,
where there was less place for these skills in a more advanced
technological society.

Dropped out as they have been for centuries, Gypsies have
recently been compared to hippies (both called 'unclean' in a
society revering cleanliness next to Godliness); being all
diaspora, to Jews ('Gaja', Romani for non-Gypsy bears an
uncanny though probably coincidental resemblance to 'Goye',
Yiddish for non-Jew), and the service today is grudging, as
though we were Blacks. In this pub we must pant after it and
it is far from polite. Don't ask me how the waitress knows
Gratton Puxon is a Gypsy. Maybe it's his Dilko, a brightly
coloured swath of cloth around his neck like a carnival
bow-tie. Dilkos are not very popular in the Royal Borough of
Barking. 'No travellers may enter here,' says the sign by
Walmsted Flats, Puxon's neighbourhood green.

President of the *Gypsy Council,* co-author (along with Donald
Kenrick) of *The Destiny of Europe's Gypsies,* sole author of the
pamphlet *The Rom: The Gypsies of Europe*, Puxon is a lucid, pale
young man with a high receding forehead who looks English
and feels uncomfortable living in a house: 'I went to Ireland to
avoid military service. I did not particularly want to be sent to
Cyprus to fight Greek nationalists trying to liberate
themselves from English occupation. I felt I would have been
on the wrong side . . .'

He laughs, a shy, delicate, almost anaemic, laugh: 'I keep out of the system. Maybe I shouldn't be saying this but . . . I don't pay taxes. Gypsies don't take anything out of the system and as far as possible we don't put anything in . . . '

'Has there ever been a Gypsy system . . . a Gypsy homeland?'

'There has been a movement for the establishment of a Gypsy state, called Romanistan. It was really more symbolic, as I see it, than anything else. It might be possible as a first step to set up some sort of diplomatic enclave, part of a territory of another country, with embassy status. Some of our people went to Algeria to discuss an embassy similar to the one Eldridge Cleaver and the Black Panthers had at the time. Nothing came of it. If we did establish some sort of a 'State' somewhere I would think that it would be somehow similar to the State of Israel, with say only a third of the Gypsies living there, and the bulk of them continuing their nomadic life. What we would like . . . what we need is some sort of base so that our voice can be heard in the international community . . . in the Council of Europe, in the United Nations . . . '

Puxon was educated in nine schools until the age of seventeen: 'I come from a fairly settled background. Now I'm trying to unlearn everything they taught me in their schools, that load of propaganda. You don't go to school to be educated, it's rather a sort of brainwashing, you learn to conform to society's expectations about wage-earning, patriotism and 'the rules' in general. It's just a process of training where children are suppressed and any eagerness or enthusiasm they may have is squeezed out of them. That is why Gypsies have mixed feelings about education. They don't want the State conformity that goes with learning to read and write.'

'How do you make your living?'

'I've been various things. I've poached rabbits. I've made lampshades. I travelled for several years, mostly around Ireland doing things Gypsies do and I only started living in a house eighteen months ago. Although I never went to college, I am currently researching Nazi war crimes against the Gypsies on a grant from the Jewish library in London. It seems they've run out of subjects of research related to Jews.'

The Gypsies get the dregs, society's garbage, near which they also live. We move to Johnny Connors's caravan parked hard by the Beckton Sewage Treatment Works, far-east London. The dumps, home of the Romani nation. Early afternoon, Johnny is still in bed. So are Kathleen and their four kids, all in the same bed, keeping warm. The kids' noses are running from the temperature in the unheated caravan. Johnny has slept with his daytime shirt and tie on. He needs a shave. The children tease each other and their parents and are teased. Johnny finally gets out and starts his day with a glass of apple wine. 'Great stuff. Made it myself.' Then he coughs for a while. 'Damn Capstan fags doin' in me troat.'

Johnny has deep lines on his face, which is nevertheless tanned and youthful, reflecting a certain kind of hick handsomeness and God-given intelligence that reminds me of the singer Johnny Cash, and I tell him so.

'Funny you should say that.' He pours wine all around. 'A man told me the same thing just the other day. And me grandfather was called Johnny-Cash-the-piper. He was a legend in his day, born in Dublin just like me. I'd like to know more about this other Johnny Cash. Haven't got the time now though, probably won't until Christmas is over, stop all this foolin' around and start, you know, puttin' in for the winter.'

It is typical of Gypsies, not puttin' in for the winter till Christmas. Take each day as it comes, each season. Johnny spent last winter in jail. It went like this. Walsall, a hard place on travellers . . . the Connors' caravan pulled over on a wide spot in the road. Kathleen putting the kids to bed. Johnny out somewhere. Pub closing time. The local constabulary bangs on the caravan door with a summons. Kathleen refuses to open up, offering instead to take the paper through the window. They break the door in, knocking her down with it. Just then Johnny returns and there is a scuffle. He is booked for assault. Kathleen goes to the hospital in an ambulance.

'Bleedin' balo . . . ' Johnny finishes the tale. 'Balo' is Scottish Gypsy argot for cop. It means, literally, 'pig', has for centuries. Johnny got ten months.

Johnny's story smells like the kind he would tell any Gajo, a judge for example. He knows what to expect from a Gajo in occupied territory. Guilt or innocence has little to do with it.

77

Like some revolutionary American rhetoric of the 'sixties, this tale of persecution is based on fact whether or not the particular is an exaggeration. The truth is the occupation, a situation, an attitude; the 'lie' an exaggeration of a specific. As if it would have changed anything in America if George Jackson had in fact killed that prison guard at Soledad, as if he didn't have more than enough provocation. A particular fiction is constructed on the white lie of abused innocence, we have perhaps not been told the entire story. What has Johnny done to provoke the balo? However, if we begin to dig into it we must dig still deeper and understand what centuries of official provocation can do to a minority. The truth is that Jews do tend to be money changers, for example, the lie to omit saying that society long denied them other means of making a living. The truth is that Gypsies do lie and steal and are dirty, the lie to omit stating the causes . . . that they are only permitted to stop next to garbage dumps, that society in general forced them to the periphery and thus to peripheral activities.

The occupation of the Gypsies has been so brutal and permanent that after as many as half a million vanished in Nazi camps, not one Gypsy witness was called by the prosecution at the Nuremberg War Crimes Trials.[2] After the war, the Gypsies who survived Auschwitz refused to give details about their families:

> They were reluctant to impart any information even for indemnification claims which could be used to trace and detain relations because they suspected *persecution would recommence* . . . There could be no guarantee that the claim forms would not be scrutinized by police agencies. Some of the single survivors and orphaned children soon fell into difficulties under the military occupation authorities and the new German civil law. Anyone who lost their displaced persons card or whose records in the UN relief agency archives had been misplaced or who had served a term in prison for any offence could be refused the papers they needed after release. In this situation when next picked up by the police, they were liable to deportation on a court order or would simply be

told on police authority to quit Germany. Some Gypsies, unable to obtain admission to another state became caught in a vicious circle, were re-imprisoned and served further terms . . .[3]

To a Gypsy, then, the new Germany and the old, the good and the bad Germans, the left and the right are not too different.

Gypsy nationalism first took shape when the Gypsy Federation was formed in Roumania in 1935. There has been a growing awareness of the need for a homeland, particularly since the war. Here is a nation unrepresented on any world council, although the Council of Europe did study the Gypsy problem, stating: 'It is a sad reflection that surviving Gypsies who were the victims of Nazi crimes – contrary to various other groups who suffered severely during World War II – have received only a negligible official compensation for the brutality inflicted on them.'[4]

When Jean-Paul Sartre's prestigious radical review, *Les Temps Modernes,*[5] published a fat, comprehensive issue on every minority in France there was one minor omission, the Gypsies. The European Federalists, a tenuous grouping of ethnics which represents every national minority not otherwise represented, does not represent the Gypsies.

For a while there was a possibility of a piece of land in Slovakia, where there are more than 250,000 Gypsies. Talks had been under way with the Dubcek regime before the Russian invasion. They were suspended. Marshall Tito once considered giving Gypsies a token region – just enough to be admitted to the club – of Macedonia to where many had fled from the Nazis and where many had fought with Tito's partisans, but the idea was shelved until 1968 when the Gypsy Union, which had been banned, was allowed to re-form and resumed agitating. There are now Macedonian schools which teach in Romani, and Suto Orizari, near Skopje, has a Gypsy mayor and M.P.

Leulea Rouda, insurance executive in majority style suit and tie opens his brief-case and pulls out papers pertaining to his second profession as General Secretary of the World Romani Congress, based in Paris.

' . . . The Gypsies of the world constitute one people with a common culture, background, history and language and a traditional way of life which is no way inferior to any other. We demand that a Gypsy be given the right to become the citizen of the country in which he resides subject to the laws and regulations governing that citizenship. Until that is accomplished, we ask the United Nations or some other international body to study the possibilities of providing all Gypsies with a personal identification and travel document enabling them to travel freely from one place to another as anyone else is allowed freely to travel. We demand . . . '

The World Romani Congress was born in Paris in 1962. This French base set up sections in other European countries, building on loose associations of clans already existing. Leulea Rouda: 'Actually, we are living in a period of renaissance. Young Gypsies no longer want to leave the tribe for life in the majority culture. In the tribe we do not know mental illness, that is not a Gypsy disease. It is only when a Gypsy leaves his family that he becomes unbalanced, begins to drink, et cetera. Young Gypsies see that now, they stay with their families now, speak their language, fight for their rights. The larger society is clearly falling apart and the Gypsies are retreating back into their families. We think this is one solution to the great social problems of our time. Politically, the Gypsies have always been ephemeral, whenever there was an obstacle of some kind, some sort of trouble, the Roms would try and disappear somewhere, but this is no longer possible, there is no longer room to disappear, so we are organizing.'

Meanwhile, the Gypsies remain . . . occupied. In Russia, though they posesss nominal nationality, only 134,000 of the 400,000 Romani population have declared themselves, the remainder register as Russian or Armenian or Georgian and so on.[6] At most, 10% remain nomadic. A 1956 law outlawing nomadism is not enforced and many Gypsies travel from one collective farm to another providing needed seasonal labour. Most, however, stay underground.

In Italy, the police staged many raids on the Roms.[7] In October 1969, they surrounded a camp in Centocelle, near Rome airport, where hundreds were roused from their sleep and loaded on to paddy wagons. Their papers were checked and half were ordered back to their place of origin, distant villages where there was neither work nor family. Sixteen were deported. Only one was found 'guilty' of anything, a misdemeanour.

Until 1970, Belgium officially maintained that there were no Gypsies in Belgium.[8] The police have instructions to prevent nomads from entering the country and, as by law even Belgian-born Gypsies are aliens, it could thus be said that indeed, legally speaking, there were no Belgian Gypsies. Families are allowed to park only a maximum of twenty-four hours along the roads. Longer stays near garbage dumps are sometimes tolerated. Gypsy infant mortality rate is 20% above the national average.

In West Germany, official policy is basically limited to confining semi-settled families and forlorn individuals left over from the Nazi period in some forty dilapidated camps.[9] A few are actually on the same sites as former concentration camps. And there are still some Stateless Gypsies, most of whom are the grown children of refugees, born without papers. Technically, they are liable to deportation but, as no other country is willing to accept them and nobody really cares enough to pursue the matter, the law remains inoperable.

In France, nomadic Gypsies are required to carry a 'Carnet de circulation' which is constantly checked by the police.[10] The law (January 3rd, 1969) stipulates that the Préfet of each Department has the right to decide to which municipality nomads must become officially attached. The Council of Europe report points out that other French citizens have the freedom to choose their place of residence. The same law disenfranchises those who cannot prove three years' unbroken residence in one place. The French Government has from time to time issued directives suggesting, but not ordering that local authorities set up caravan camping sites for nomads. Less than a dozen responded and existing legal camping grounds are usually on wasteland next door to garbage dumps.

In England, the dumps again.

Mary, a pudgy lady with skin suffering from an overdose of fish and chips, pours tea in her caravan parked behind the

Connors'. 'Do you have travellers in America, like here in England?'

'Yes, but many people live in trailers in America so they are harder to spot.'

'You got slums over there, like we got here?'

'Yes. Mostly black people in them though.'

'Is it? Well black *and* white live in 'em here, don't they? I always thought America was a rich country. And yet there are slum people who got nothin'. How come?'

'Like here. Ten per cent of the people own ninety per cent of the country.'

'Johnny here's one of the ten per cent. Got all the money . . .'

'Oh yea . . . ' Johnny Connors has just poked his head through Mary's door. 'I own ninety per cent of this here two bob. Hey! Old Harry just told me that they arrested Dobie Chapman for campin' on the highway down in Kent.'

'Oh me!' Mary sighs. 'Guess *we'll* soon be kicked on our way too. No place to stop any more, not even by the dumps. We're like bloody fugitives, we are.'

Five
Bevet Breiz[1]

'You can't organize this place like the others.' –
Major-domo of Brittany (1703)

A Conglomerate Motel, the heart of the beast. Monyglot
modernity behind mass-produced turf on the outskirts.
Unmusical Muzak, three-decker clubs, synthetic carpets,
sanitized toilets . . . multi-national castles featuring jet-lag
and motorway hypnosis. Pale people in purple lobbies with
carry-on bags, putrid drapes in perfumed fortresses. It's
embarrassing.

Here I am researching a book on national minorities, on the
crest of a new nationalism that has at its centre the will to
remain different, minority cultures fighting a last-ditch battle
to defend themselves against this very beast which eats the
same food, watches the same images, listens to the same
sounds, wears the same clothes, governs with the same
inhuman inefficiency . . . this multi-national sinister
conglomeration called internationalism. Researching the
small, the old, the individual, why have I checked into the
Conglomerate?

Will you believe me if I say the other hotels were all booked?
No? What if I say they were too small, noisy or overpriced?
Not that either? Okay, how about a weak side? I have had my
share of pissing in bed-and-breakfast sinks.

So I soak in Conglomerate bath foam, free in a little packet
like some sample of dope from the neighbourhood pusher.
Aahh . . . I have adjusted my very own personal thermostat
and as soon as I get out, if ever, I will order a steak from room
service. This is the life.

Soaking, I decide the Conglomerate is not in bad taste
really, more an absence of taste, literally no taste to the place.
No past and not much of a future . . . the plaster is already

peeling around the edge of the tub. A personality designed to insult absolutely nobody, in other words no personality at all. An absence of flavour. When the French lecture the Bretons: 'You are *French*, not Breton,' they really mean: 'You are *American*.' The French are no longer capable of defending their culture against American colonialism, or rather it is no longer either American or French or anything else other than monyglot. The French would certainly not like to hear that they no longer have any culture of their own, they are not aware of it, at least consciously, surely not prepared to admit it if they are, but still the evidence is overwhelming. At least it seems overwhelming here in this tub. We are all soaking in multi-national bath foam, trying to forget the rot outside. The Conglomerate appeals to the same weak side which allows us to accept MORE as an ethic, which says slow is bad, fast is good, big is better, poor is inferior and minorities are minor. The weak side on which States run. We wallow in our weak side.

The foam flattens, my skin crinkles. Dial 9 for a steak. Make several phone calls (direct dial) for appointments tomorrow. Smoke a joint.

Marijuana, muggles, pot, grass . . . once itself a symbol of protest against THE SAME. Let those squares out there get sloppy drunk, not us, this is something you cannot control although you try to occupy my very body with guilt for victimless crime. I claimed my freedom of the 'pursuit of happiness' long ago from a presumptuous State. But here too THE SAME has caught up with me. Every advertising executive and lawyer worth his Martini now smokes grass in America and America exported marijuana just like *Perry Mason* (which is on my enamelled swivel-pivot receiver at the moment). *Easy Rider* turns out to be nothing but cultural imperialism. But old habits are hard to shed (I would not object to your calling it a habit) and although it is no longer the symbol of anything I am totally smashed in my sealed cage when one of tomorrow's appointments rings on the house phone. He has had a change of schedule and fell by on the off-chance I might be free tonight.

Free? Tonight?

Sober up! Get your act together. Open the window. Wash

your face. Brush your hair. Collect some questions. Check out the tape recorder. Think in French. Time for some serious conversation in the lobby of the Conglomerate.

'Would you like some snuff?'

Snuff? Where are we? What year is this? Who is this? I'll call him Hardy, this red-faced man with fertile head of prematurely grey hair, overweight, wearing a black turtle-neck, extending a small, polished wooden canister. My records show he is a member of the Parti Communiste Breton. A Communist? Snuff?

He pours some brown powder on the hollow between my thumb and forefinger. Just the ticket to clear out the muggles. 'What do you think about the transmitter affair?'

One week before my arrival the French State television transmitter in Roc-Tredudon, Western Brittany, was blown up by the Front de Libération de la Bretagne (F.L.B.).

There have been over fifty explosions in Brittany since 1966. The Prefect of Côtes-du-Nord, one department of Brittany (Brittany does not exist, it is five departments of France) said: 'Nothing but a mess provoked by some retarded students,' although among the eighty suspects arrested there were more farmers, workers and priests than students. While there is not much open support for blowing up the transmitter, neither is there general disapproval. The F.L.B. is composed of less than a hundred militants whose techniques have the admiration of specialists like the I.R.A. Some say they are trained by the I.R.A. They work on railways, fishing boats, in canning factories. They blow something up on Saturday night, and Monday morning they are back on the shop floor. They are no media freaks, they know how to disappear. They are hard to catch and so, lacking the individuals, the French Government banned the organization which gave it more importance than it deserved. The Breton autonomist movement has been on the front pages for weeks now. There are more than the usual number of French police on the roads, checking the papers of ordinary folks, and some ordinary folks are beginning to say that if there isn't a Breton liberation movement maybe there should be.

'What transmitter affair? I never heard of any affair. You heard anything about a transmitter?' Hardy turns to his companion, just trailing into the lobby behind him. 'Laurel' is thin and short and keeps scratching the top of his head with his fingertips in puzzlement, a mannerism which, together with the obese joviality of his companion, reminds me of the famed comic duo.

'Me. Not me,' says Laurel, rolling his eyes. He is wearing serious walking boots with mud caked on them and a torn leather jacket. He scratches his head again, takes a sniff of snuff and pretends to pick his nose as Hardy tries to turn serious: '. . . As they say, it doesn't mean anything to own the universe if you lose your own soul . . . ' I have the distinct impression that he is trying to sober up for *me* . . . 'We say that when you destroy the soul of a people, you destroy their capacity to create, to construct a viable society. When you hide their present from them, destroy their cultural inheritance, you make it impossible for a people to construct their future . . . ' Laurel holds up two fingers like horns behind Hardy's head . . . 'That's what has been happening here. The history of Brittany is forbidden, systematically camouflaged, we are taught only French history with the objective of making everybody as French as possible. The Breton heritage is systematically hidden from us. This is what we call the colonialization of the spirit . . . '

Hardy catches Laurel at it and gives him a hit on the head.

Laurel shakes his head, rattles it back and forth for a while and then shrugs his shoulders with a sort of mock hopelessness that says . . . what can I do? I'm in this funny movie . . .

'Oh come on,' says Hardy, after some chat and snuff-sniffing. 'We can be honest with Mike. Tell him about the transmitter. You were there after all.'

Which he does, and which is the reason I have hidden their identities. However, they have not *asked* me to hide anything and I am puzzled: 'How do you know I'm not a cop?'

'As a matter of fact the thought crossed my mind,' says Hardy, obviously not particularly bothered by it.

Laurel smiles with contentment describing the glorious explosion, the close call he had with a watchman, the planning and co-ordination it had taken to blow the transmitter up without loss of human life. 'Of course we don't expect a lot of people to understand. Television is a drug, and if you take people's drugs away they will not be happy for a while. But they'll understand. They are our people. We speak the same language.'

Hardy is quick to assure me that the P.C.B. definitely does not speak the same language as the *French* Communist Party. 'They are not amusing,' he says. 'Communists do not know how to smile.'

A snuff-sniffing Communist who does not approve of Communists, 'terrorists' who avoid taking human life, reckless natures, the love of a mess . . . perfect examples of the Breton character.

We move into the restaurant, a tidy, antiseptic place with a long formica counter and clothed tables along a picture window overlooking the swimming pool. I am not embarrassed any more. Laurel and Hardy are perfectly at home in these 'counter-revolutionary' surroundings, as though born to them. My excuses have already been shrugged away with: 'After the revolution, *everybody* will be able to stay here.' They order a bottle of 1966 Bordeaux and a dozen oysters each. Hardy offers a toast: 'Make love *during* war.'

The counter soon fills up with a number of straight looking students dressed formally who have come in from the ballroom on the other side of the lobby, where, our waiter tells us, the local dental school is holding its annual dance. The students are neat, conformist, very French. You might think them the classic enemy of a Breton revolutionary if you did not know Brittany. The students are giggling, with a happy buzz on and they are an attractive bunch. Having just been served a heaped bowl of mussels, one of the girls leans over to our table and looks closely at Laurel's oysters. 'Oooh, oysters,' she coos, sniffing them. "How are they?"

Laurel bats his eyes: 'I'll trade you my oyster for your mussel.' She laughs. Hardy offers her some snuff. Laurel opens Hardy's mouth and pours an oyster in it. Hardy gulps and pours some 1966 Bordeaux on Laurel's head. Two revolutionaries in the Conglomerate, the heart of the beast, the heart of THE SAME, which we are beginning to understand is not the same in Brittany.

Around midnight, they excuse themselves for leaving so early. There are revolutionary posters to paste up around town. Then they must be up at six for the factory. I look at my watch: 'You don't sleep much, do you?'

'No. But we sleep *well*.'

A weird map arrived in the mail; odd, unreal chunks of land with names as unfamiliar as Occitania. It was titled, hopefully:

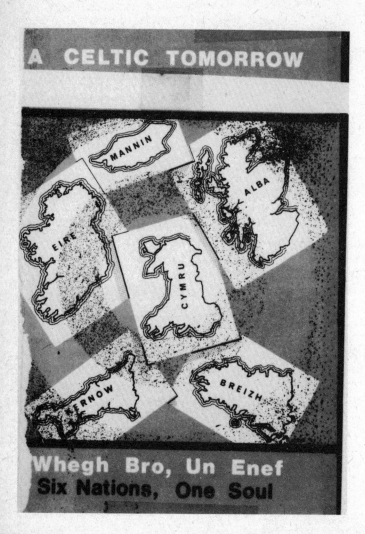

The Celtic archipelago. Odd lumps of land meaning little to mainstream twentieth-century civilization. The Isle of Man, Scotland, Cornwall, Ireland, Wales and Brittany . . . vestiges of an ancient race and a high culture still amazingly held together by ties that preceded States and may just possibly survive them. Similar ties to those that held Jews together through two thousand years of diaspora, ties that go back as far as the Jews.

The Celts dominated Western Europe for a millennium, held off the Germans for centuries and twice nearly overthrew the Roman Empire.[2] The first Celts may have been the Beaker People, the people who built Stonehenge. They were followed by the Urnfielders during the Bronze age, around 1,000 B.C., so named because they burned their dead in urns. The warlike Urnfielders expanded Westwards and settled most of Gaul by 800 B.C.

Urnfielders were known for their horsemanship and introduced close-fitting trousers to Western Europe. They developed long bronze swords for slashing from horses. They built earthen forts on hill-tops, later known to the Romans as 'oppida'. Around 600 B.C. the Hallstatt culture arose when the knowledge of iron-working reached Western Europe; the name comes from Hallstatt in Austria where their most famous remains have been found. They no longer cremated their dead, and, with their new iron weapons, were aggressive warriors. They were certainly Celts. Contact with more advanced Mediterranean cultures produced the richest period of Celtic culture, the La Tène period. Classical writers described the La Tène people as tall and sturdy with a high percentage of redheads. To the Greeks they were the 'Galatae', to the Romans 'Galli', which explains the French term for Wales. 'Pays de Galles'.

In 474 B.C. the Celts descended from Alpine passes into the Po valley in what is now northern Italy where they defeated the Etruscans. They moved south and defeated the Umbrians. At the height of their power they occupied all of northern Italy and parts of France, Czechoslovakia and Roumania. In 400 B.C. the Insubre tribe founded an oppidum called Mediolanum, now Milan, while the Boli tribe renamed one they had conquered after themselves, Bologna. In 390 B.C. the

Celtic chief Brennos sacked Rome. After founding Paris, the Parisii tribe moved on to Yorkshire. The Dumnonis settled south-west England, giving name to Devon.

The Celts invaded Macedonia and occupied Thrace. They went on to defeat the Athenian Army at Thermopylae and sacked the sacred city of Delphi. They founded an oppidum, now Belgrade, and in 250 B.C. King Eumens of Greece paid them tribute to keep out of his territory.

The Celts were Druidic. The Druids were the first Europeans to claim the immortality of the soul and this, according to some classical writers, is what made them such fearless warriors. They achieved a knowledge of the planets far in advance of their Latin neighbours. The most important Celtic god was Lugos (the functions of their gods were not defined as with the Greek gods), who has left his name all over Europe, in such places as Leiden and Lyons.

The rise of Rome meant the decline of the Celts. Celtic lands south of the Alps became part of Rome, Galicia was conquered by Rome, and when many Celts fled to Britain from Armorica (Brittany) all of Gaul fell. The Celts were squeezed to death between the warlike Germans to the north and the Romans to the south.

Now a rather ragged band of survivors is trying a comeback as succeeding empires shake and fade. They send out literature calling for a 'Celtic Tomorrow'. They hold Interceltic Congresses. There were more than seven hundred Celts at the Interceltic Congress of 1974 in Nantes. Many young in T-shirts dancing and singing renaissant Celtic gavottes. There were professional ethnics such as we have already met in Wales. As in Villeneuve-sur-Lot, there was also the centralized left out to co-opt the culture. Culture, they say, is now politics. There was warmth with shared interests in mutual problems. It was more serious than previous congresses but also had an air of sadness and even hopelessness because the threat of assimilation is greater than ever now, renaissance or no renaissance.

The term 'Celtic' basically refers to a language: a Celt can be defined as somebody who speaks Gaelic, Manx, Cornish, Welsh or Breton. Manx and Cornish are almost dead. The next generation or two will decide about the rest. The

Congress of 1974 noted

> . . . with regret that the Breton language remains absent from the schools of Brittany . . . consequently the Congress appeals to the British and Irish governments to intervene with all necessary vigour with the French government in the name of the Bretons and, if necessary, to impose economic sanctions to force the French to change their policy so that it will conform to the European Convention of Human Rights vis à vis the rights of nations to learn and use their mother tongue.

Nevertheless some somehow learn it, 10,000 now in private night schools, or as an elective in high school, learning it the hard way at the expense of learning something else. Amazing how cultural ties survive two thousand years of occupation. Surviving Celtic consciousness can be gleaned on a human level from an article which appeared in the Autumn 1973 issue of *Cornish Nation,* the journal of Ariel Clark, Assistant Secretary of the Cornish Wrestling Society.

The Breton Wrestling Society had invited their Cornish cousins to an 'Interceltic wrestling match' in Lochmaria-Berrien, a small village in central Brittany. The team took the Plymouth-Roscoff (Brittany) ferry 'Poseidon' on August 13th. The ferry was 'very empty'. The Cornish team was impressed by the Bretons' 'Grand Prix' style of driving and drinking. They were surprised to find that, unlike Cornish, Breton was not a dead language. They heard a 'French' family in a restaurant speak Breton to each other and to the waitress: 'The marvellous hospitality shown to us by all concerned was most heart-warming and made us feel like members of the family. And we are of course, members of the large and close *Celtic* family.'

These secondary lines in Europe, though withering, remain real enough. Breton onion-sellers sail to Wales each autumn and ride bikes from town to town selling their onions. They speak Breton, the Welsh speak Welsh and they understand each other . . . two subcultures stuck in States for four centuries with a common vocabulary tying them very much as Yiddish ties Jews. Secondary lines like the Plymouth-Roscoff ferry for example, which was 'very empty', surely the only empty ferry between England and the continent in the busy tourist month of August. Secondary lines, minor lines, empty lines, tattered lines.

When the Romans withdrew from Brittany in the sixth century, some Celtic tribes returned from Britain (thus 'Brittany'), priests and families crossing with their animals. The Council of Tours excommunicated the Breton clergy in the seventh century because they were holding mass in the home and they were travelling with their women. The Celtic church was still pagan, stressing nature – fish, trees, the sea – still holding on to elements of Druidism. For the next three hundred years English missionaries swarmed over Brittany.

Celtic Brittany was divided into small dukedoms which fought both each other and the Merovingians and Carolingians who tried to conquer them without much success. They expelled Norse invaders in the tenth century, and fought with William of Normandy in the Battle of Hastings. French and English royalty married Breton royalty for two centuries. The peninsula tried to stay neutral in the fourteenth and fifteenth centuries but when Duke Francis II died without a male heir in 1488, his daughter, Anne, married Charles VIII of France; Anne's daughter Claude married Francis I who concluded the treaty of 1532 which attached Brittany to France just four years before Wales was attached to England.

The Bretons were promised their own courts, their own assembly, the right to raise and spend their own taxes. But, as a North American Indian was to say three hundred years later: 'The white man kept only one promise. He promised to take our land and he took it.'

A little old lady sits in a little old house in Mur-de-Bretagne, a little old town in the centre of the peninsula. I was advised not to bother to see her. 'Only folklorique,' the adviser said. She sits amidst piles of books, newspapers, bulletins and in-and-out mail. There is a duplicator, several big old typewriters, all to one purpose. To advertise a four-century-old treaty which has been broken and just about forgotten except for one promise. The French promised to occupy Brittany and they occupied it.

A task doomed to ridicule. People who remind us of old broken promises tend to be accused of sour grapes. They remind us of flaws in our system, our institutions, ourselves. They are good for an occasional short 'local colour' piece on the back page of the Sunday paper. They are folklorique.

Mademoiselle Kerhuel, a spunky little lady in sensible shoes, cranking out a monthly newsletter pushing the treaty of 1532. She has a doctorate in political economy and is retired now after working twenty years in the French Ministry of Economic Affairs. Hey everybody, look at the funny old Indian sitting in the teepee trying to sell us a used treaty: 'The treaty of 1532 is the only title the French State has to Brittany . . .' She cackles between sentences like an animated hen, adding another irony to the irony . . . 'When one party wants to preserve the advantages of a contract without fulfilling its obligations, any court would condemn him. This, however, is what the French State has been doing with us for two hundred years. If we could simply go back to the conditions under which we accepted to join the French State, which were agreed to under the treaty of 1532 . . .'

The Jacobins clamped terminal centralization on France right after the revolution. The provinces often remained monarchist and reactionary and centralization was the progressive way. The Girondins, being in favour of maintaining provincial autonomy, were reactionary. The Girondins' defeat was a victory for the people. 'Girondin' is still an insult in France. Although, with the plain inefficiency of centralization becoming impossible for anybody to ignore, there has lately been some lip-service regionalization. Twenty-two regions have been set up in between the ninety-five departments and the State. These are, however, arbitrary (Nantes, for example, its natural capital, is cut off from Brittany), powerless (no legislative duties), poor (an annual budget of about 20 francs – approximately £2 – per person) and not very 'regional' since the assemblies and their leaders are appointed by Paris. Another example of regionalization French-style is the third, 'regional', television channel. Each region is supposed to have its own production outfits and staff, but the reality is that everybody still has to go to Paris to get anything done and in fact most of the staff still *live* in Paris and go to Lyon or Lille, for example, for their 'regional' programmes two or three days a week.

In the nineteenth century any schoolchild caught speaking Breton wore a 'Simbol', while in Occitania it was the 'Signal' and in Wales the 'Welsh Not'. The Industrial Revolution emptied the Breton countryside in favour of Paris. The Industrial Revolution never really reached Brittany, due largely to the high price of coal which Paris forced the Bretons to take by rail from the Lorraine. The policies of Paris were oriented towards the good of Paris and the idea of the Bretons' natural supplier, their cousins the Welsh, shipping coal by boat at a fraction of the price was not only ignored but was considered positively unpatriotic.

There were 400,000 Bretons living in Paris by the end of the nineteenth century. After reaching a maximum of 2,600,000 in 1911, the population of the peninsula fell to 2,300,000 during World War II and has risen to about 3,000,000 now, of whom it is estimated half a million still speak their language. Three hundred and fifty thousand still live in Paris.

The Parti Nationaliste Breton (P.N.B.) was formed in 1912, with the motto: 'With France if possible, without it if necessary.' In 1919, Olivier Mordrel took the motto further with his 'Breiz Atao' (Brittany Forever) which was more aggressively anti-French, its platform calling for a free Brittany within a federated Europe. Mordrel's idea of 'Celtic purity' bore certain unfortunate similarities to what Hitler was saying at the same time. Mordrel supported Hitler in 1936, for which he was condemned to a year in jail by the Daladier government. He slipped across the border, however, and began issuing statements assuring the Bretons of Hitler's support. After Germany occupied France and some Breton autonomists began strutting about in Nazi uniforms, it became apparent that this was only another even more odious occupation and the 'French' underground was as active in Brittany as anywhere else.

Pro-Nazi sentiment in Brittany can be explained as a schizophrenic aberration caused by centuries of exploitation, similar to sentiment at the same time in Ireland. World War II national schizophrenia was even more acute in Alsace and perhaps this is a good time to jump across to the eastern frontier of France and discuss this much pummelled nation.

Alsace was ceded by France to Germany in 1871, receded to France in 1911, annexed by Hitler in 1940 and recovered by France in 1945. It is now three departments of France. Legally speaking, that geographic and national entity known as Alsace does not exist.

Unlike Brittany, Alsace is no corner. It has been conquered by everybody, starting with Caesar, and it is a miracle that any Alsatian consciousness exists at all ... particularly since the language (which has more than a dozen dialects) resembles German and to speak a language resembling German in France leaves the speaker open to cultural derision if not persecution.

Raymond Poincaré banned all newspapers in Alsatian and German in 1925 even though German was the mother-tongue of more than half the population. There were searches, seizures and arrests. An autonomist named Eugene Ricklin called for complete autonomy 'within the French State', while the French Government maintained that autonomist sentiment was treason. Alsatians kept electing autonomists to the French Chamber of Deputies and a precarious balance was maintained until Hitler upset it.

On August 25th, 1942, in an Alsace now 'liberated' by the Germans, a decree was published ordering military service in the German Army for any Alsatian born between 1920 and 1922. The mobilization was later expanded to include over 100,000 Alsatians. If anybody resisted, their families were taken as hostages. Just as the Communists sent the anarchists to the most dangerous battle-zones in the Spanish civil war, the Germans used the Alsatian division in Stalingrad.

The division is known as the 'Malgré Nous' (Despite Us). There were mass desertions towards the end of the war, though the Soviets, not particularly versed or interested in the subtleties of Fourth World culture, put the deserters in concentration camps which were not very different from those of the Nazis.

The war silenced the Alsatian autonomist movement as it silenced that in Brittany – with the accusation of pro-Nazi. It was a more lasting and heavy accusation though since the

Alsatian nation had only recently belonged to Germany and many of them still spoke German. Many still speak it. The French do not like people who speak German.

In fact the French do not really like anybody but the French, when you get down to it. They certainly cannot understand how a 'Frenchman' could want to be anything but French. It is an attitude one might call 'colonial'.

The Breton autonomist movement began to regain credibility fifteen years after the end of the war with the formation of the 'Union Democratique Bretonne' (U.D.B.) out of the ashes of the P.N.B., with the marriage of nationalism with socialism.

Schism begat schism until by 1972 there were some ten separate and distinct tendencies on the Breton left, the most militant and least visible being the F.L.B. The F.L.B. was dismantled in 1972 after one last caper against the residence of a certain François Bouygues who had been 'convicted' of unBreton real-estate development. Eleven of its members were tried for terrorism and seeking to overthrow the authority of the State.

As the trial began, Dr Yves Gourvés, one of the accused, requested an interpreter through his lawyer because he said he did not speak French. The prosecution objected: 'The defendant speaks and understands French perfectly. Otherwise how could he have finished his medical studies?'

'He forgot his French in jail,' said the defence.

The judge asked Gourvés if he had anything to say.

'Ne gomzin nemet e brezhoveg,' replied the doctor.

The defendants did not deny the charges. Their lawyers said they were no anarchists but responsible nationalists forced to violence by an intransigent State. They were fighting for just ends . . . the right to speak their language, the right to a local assembly, to spend their own taxes. The defence called members of other ethnic movements. Michel Mayol, a young Catalan lawyer said: 'These men reacted in legitimate self-defence against cultural alienation, economic exploitation and colonialism. The defendants are not desperados as they have been depicted, but the hope of Brittany. Oppressive conditions provoke resistance.'

The word 'resistance' is still magic in France, recalling as it does *The* Resistance during that most famous and indisputable of modern occupations, the German. French Resistance hero General Jacques Paris de Bolladière testified: 'The actions these Bretons are accused of I myself committed during the resistance.'

> Potatoes for the pigs,
> peelings for the Bretons . . .
> (French children's song)

A radical journalist and theatre critic for *La Canard Enchaîné* named Morvan Lebesque discovered he was Breton not French and in 1970 published a book about it.[3] It was the same sort of discovery that Georges Lapassade was to make some years later, and that John Jenkins made about the same time. (Compare the following with Jenkins's prison letters on page 66.)

I had taken to Brittany illegally, secretly. She was only my common law wife. She was my sin, my whore. But I can testify, after so many years and now that we are both old, that the unmentionable liaison has made me deeply happy.

My century appeared to me in its true colours, it would be that of the resurgence of ethnic groups and not of their disappearance . . . In this new world contract, it was logical that Brittany should find her place, crushed though she still was under nineteenth century dogmas. But the essential – the defence of her personality – would no longer be an idea of the right, but of the left, and only this revolution would offer to France a chance of true democracy.

Brittany came out of the war bled-white. Twice-French indeed, 240,000 dead, twice as many proportionally as in the rest of France. Sacrificed because rural, and rural because sacrificed.

There is an overproduction of artichokes near St Pol-de-Léon. The farmers go to Paris every year to beg for customers in the street. Last year while they were there a shipping line that transports bananas from Dakar to Le Havre and returns empty had the idea of taking artichokes back. They tried to reach the farmers' co-operative to set up a deal but there was no answer because the farmers were all in Paris begging for customers. A country which is bordered on three sides by water is forced to live by its one with land. If Brazil buys Renault tractors in exchange for agricultural products, Brazilian agriculture products flood France and Breton farmers get poorer. If Holland buys French cars in exchange for Dutch butter, the market is flooded with Dutch butter and the price of Breton butter tumbles. If France sneezes, Brittany gets a cold.

Except for its rather spooky, Druidic interior, Brittany does not look poor. The houses are clean, there are many new ones, roads are good, there are occasional new factories. Some French authorities even speak of a boom, though a boom on the periphery is always several notches less than one at the centre. To find the base of the movement we must look at the spirit of the people. The Breton movement is largely incomprehensible to the French because their Cartesian nature has to *explain* everything. They demand analytical logic and it is necessary above all to avoid analysing the Bretons. To analyse them is to confess not to understand them. They are not logical. Communists who think Communists don't laugh enough. 'S.A.V.', a 'right-wing' autonomist group which says they follow the Anarchist Bakunin. A 'folklorique' little old lady who is much more than folklore. The French cannot understand anything they cannot categorize and so they prefer to say there is no Breton problem. While the Bretons say, we prefer to be crazy the way we are rather than intelligent the way you are.

'WARNING! The French secret police are following you.' We are in the rectory of the village of Gommenec'h. Father Love the Breton has just pulled the warning out of his wallet. 'You see.' He looks grave. 'We have *our* police too.'

Father Love the Breton (Aimé le Breton) is his real name. I did not make it up. It is part of the ambiance.

I apologize to the father: 'Pardon my French. I have a lot of trouble with French.'

'Oh it's all right, so do I.' We are not in France here. Politically perhaps, but that is a situation soon, the father hopes, to be rectified; the Bretons are about as French as Indians are American. They look French, they speak French, but scratch the surface a bit and you will find a Breton. 'If you had come eight days ago you would have found ten cops on my tail.'

Or was it ten days and eight cops. I sense exaggeration. No matter, one cop is enough: 'It was very funny. I love to play their game. I did a hundred and twenty on some back roads I know better than they do, believe me, and I finally shook them.'

Le Breton would like to go to jail. He tells everybody – Norwegian television, Danish television, me – everybody, what an honour it is for a Breton to go to a French jail. He was arrested at a demonstration five years ago for three days – or was it three years ago for five days? – and it was his golden hour. ('I only spoke to them in Breton. They had to get a translator.') The journalist who touted me on le Breton said he would be good for 'folklore'. The father fancies himself as a revolutionary, said the journalist, but he talks too much. Nothing is clear in Brittany, however, and as with Mlle Kerhuel we learn that even folklore is more than folklore in Brittany. There is something very special going on and a paranoid militant priest by the name of Love the Breton is not the least of it.

Brown furrowed, grey fringe combed back, wearing a green cord suit and black crew-neck sweater, his hands always moving in a tic of emphasis, Love the Breton seems more like an Irish revolutionary than a French priest: 'The Bretons are religious people. They are close to nature, concrete, realists. They believe in what they can see and feel . . . trees, sheep, their land, the sea, home, family. A Frenchman can be on the left because the *ideas* of the left appeal to him. It does not work that way in Brittany. We must *feel* injustice before we will react to it. That is why I do not condemn this transmitter affair . . . '

Le Breton once more digs in his wallet for a clandestine goodie, this time a communiqué signed 'F.L.B.': '. . . for the creation of an autonomous socialist republic of Brittany.'

You can bet the French Government fixed that transmitter fast. Not to lose too much propaganda. The Bretons had reacted like junkies in need of a fix. For two weeks, Brittany had been the only place in the western world without the eye; people were really lost for a while, they had to talk to each other over dinner, and the French press had been full of talk about useless and counter-productive violence. But a lot of French police had been rushed to Brittany and they were highly visible and all of a sudden occupation became just that much more tangible: 'It is necessary to awaken the Breton people on a very basic level to the fact that they have been brutalized, victimized, colonialized. It is the only way they will ever awake. And television is a good symbol to attack, a symbol of how we have all become robots, all pressed down by this gigantic modernism. People want more and more to take refuge from it, to move back from it towards something they can understand. This is what the current renaissance of national minorities is all about.'

The renaissance is more obvious in Brittany than in Wales. They are dancing. In any town of any size on any weekend there is a public party, a 'Fest Noz', where chains of Bretons dance gavottes, arms linked, holding hands, jumping and skipping as the chain winds. The chain is more important than individual style. Transmitting energy, love, support, three generations intertwined. The music they dance to is in full bloom, ancient Celtic musical traditions having been brought to contemporary pop charts principally through Alan Stivell, who heads bills at Olympia, and who has toured England and the States.

Here, now, in the city hall of Maël-Carhaix, an exotic mixture of a *biniou* (Breton bag-pipes), *bombards* (small, recorder-like flutes), two electric guitars, a violin, an electric flute and tom-toms. The accordionist looks as though he would have collaborated with the Germans: clipped, erect, tense. He is standing next to the electric flutist, who is wearing beads, white Indian trousers, an Afghani vest and has hair far down his back. They are smiling at each other, playing gavottes in odd meters like three threes and a four, or fives or sevens . . . smiling at each other to beat the band. Farmers, businessmen, artists, politicians . . . young and old, right and left, skip and jump to the odd meters as though born to them, which of course they all were. Rhythms awkward, even indecipherable to a non-Celt, to somebody from the centre where we dance without touching each other to a pounding uniform monybeat . . . one one one one . . . and you can see at any Fest Noz what we lack at the centre . . . lack three threes and a four if you will, something unique together, the ability to link arms and hold hands and dance regardless of any other differences there may be between us.

Across the road, in the type of tabac you see all over France, some people are sitting and drinking as they do all over the world. Passing lonely evenings with television over the whisky bottles. Not looking at each other, nothing to say, nothing better to do, avoiding going home. Many of them are staring into space, only a few speak to each other. The conversations are short and, from what I can overhear, far from communicative. A void, no contact, nothing to hope for; a coin in the juke-box . . . Mick Jagger sings:

> Angie . . . Angie . . .
> Where will it lead to from here . . .?

Sitting and drinking thinking of somewhere else, wondering where it will lead to from here. The contrast with the joyful integrated Fest Noz across the road is what Nationism is all about.

Back in Gommenec'h, the sun sets through the open window of the rectory. The temperature in the room brings smoke from the mouth of Father Love the Breton who is only warming up. The Bretons love to talk even more than the French, which means a lot. He talks about aspects of Brittany already covered here, about the culture, the language, economics. But most of all he talks politics. He refers to the I.R.A. and E.T.A. without really ever referring to them. He refers to 'they' and 'one' and 'somebody' for an hour. I am not sure who he means, or whether *he* is sure. This however is clear enough: 'My parish thinks I go too far. They do not yet understand that we are fighting for survival. The people are not yet ready to fight. But they will be. I know my people. A neighbour said to me the other day: "Father, I do not approve of everything you say, but I love you anyway." '

Six
Hotinonsionne[1]

'I felt that I had visited a world as different from the
United States as any foreign country, and I began to see
upstate New York, all my life so familiar to me, in a new
and larger perspective.' – Edmund Wilson: *Apologies to the
Iroquois*

Red Stone walked out of a Broadway book store and saw a
hawk. The hawk made several slow, gliding circles and
suddenly broke out due north. Hawks do not generally fly
around the middle of a city like that. Red knew a sign when he
saw one.

Ploughing through radical periodicals in the book store, he
had stumbled across an ad in *Akwesasne Notes,* published by
'The Great White Roots of Peace', a commune on a Mohawk
reservation astride the Canadian border. ' . . . We need a
housepainter . . . room and board . . . '

Bizarre. Why should Red want to paint a house? Yet he
knew when he read it that it was directed at him. He had felt
for a long time now that contemporary society was using
outdated forms of communication – words for instance. Words
are merely accessories after the fact. Real communication is
telepathic. He had learned that from his first dog back on the
farm in Tennessee. Maybe he would follow the hawk north.

Red had always felt marginal, occupied, an outsider;
unconventional at least. He had become a hipster naturally,
effortlessly, without even thinking about it, after having heard
Charlie Parker for the first time. He understood what freedom
meant immediately and knew he could never work 9-5 like
other people. He worked harder than any nine-to-fiver and
took more risks and was often suffocated by his vocation but
there remained at least an illusion of freedom. In short, he
mistook alienation for freedom.

Red pushed coke in Philly, grass in Baltimore, had a string
of hookers in New York. He ran orgies at the Pierre. He took

nothing out of what he considered a corrupt system and put nothing in. But it was money and consumption first and for a long time he did not see he was only living the American dream inside out.

One day Red put too much coke up his nose and flashed that inside-out or not he was still living the American dream and that he had not spoken to anybody but gangsters in a week.

He was doing his best to bop around MacDougal Street when he heard an old cough down a hole. He looked down to see this wreck of a man carrying up a load of coal. The man coughed a lot more when he hit the sidewalk. What kind of shitty world is this, Red thought. Here I am with nothing to do, twenty-five hundred cash in my pocket, young, healthy . . . and look at that old man. It don't make no sense.

Then he saw the hawk. Red had never lost his country-boy awareness of messages brought by nature. While shacked up with a fifteen-year-old nymphomaniac in the California woods, he had been on intimate terms with a few redwoods who lived nearby. He told his top hooker Cheryl he was beginning to freak out and that maybe he should go and live with the Indians for a while.

'Sure, baby,' she said, painting her toe-nails. 'Sure, you go do that.'

For those who may be wondering what an American Indian chapter is doing in a book about European Nationism, let me explain. It seems to me that Nationism actually began when Jeff Chandler starred in a movie sometime in the 'fifties, *Broken Arrow*, playing a good Indian. In that movie, the good guys suddenly became the bad guys and vice versa, and we began to see history in a mirror. Massacres became glorious victories, glorious victories massacres. 'Progressive' Indians – those who want to live like Whites – became reactionary and the 'Traditionals' – keeping to the old ways – became progressive. Through the media the American Indian has become perhaps the best known example of a nation occupied by a State. They make a good reference point.

I flew up to Montreal, rented a car and drove back over the border which makes 'Americans' and 'Canadians' out of

Mohawks to Nation House, a plain, squat, white-frame structure fronted by a screened porch with bales of newspapers leaving only a narrow aisle to walk through. The house was buzzing with dark young people, many with coloured headbands, beads and ponytails ... sorting, stacking, rolling and pasting the latest issue of *Akwesasne Notes*. I was put in Red Stone's care. Two hipsters on the reservation.

Once upon a time a hippy was a square hipster. 'Stupid hippies,' we used to say. Hippies were squares trying to act hip, which was worse than square. Hipsters and hippies had the same idol, Charlie Parker, though hippies only listened to him because he was 'hip'. Hipsters played jazz, hippies were the greasers banging bongos, messing up the time. Hipsters debauched in homage to Poe and Baudelaire ... hippies were just bums like their old man. Hippies dropped out because they were too dumb or lazy to do anything else, while for hipsters it was a political decision. Hipsters discovered Black argot and Black man's dope before they were fashionable, our clothes were odd and scoffed, we were hairy for the time, our music was the only truth we cared about and our parents neither understood nor approved. We slouched around, hunched forward, one hand in a pocket, eyes red, cradling horns in leather sacks, wearing goatees and Dizzy Gillespie berets. Those of us who weren't junkies scratched our noses to look like we were.

Red and I had both survived the hazards of this ethic and came out the other side along with the amelioration of hippy. We saw the secrets, joys, values and mistakes of our close little community co-opted by the counter-culture of the 'sixties and later by the main culture itself. When 'cool' showed up in *Time*, when hair reached shoulders on Madison Avenue, when junk appeared on Park Avenue, we realized it was time to move somewhere else. I moved to Occitania, Red to Akwesasne.

My second evening in Nation House, I sat watching everybody sort, stack, roll and paste the newspaper. Nobody talked to me for hours. Red was upstairs painting. Strange then that I should feel so comfortable.

Somebody dropped a stapler: 'Shit!'

'Hey that's not nice. Watch your language.'

'Sorreee . . . '

It was an odd combination of a commune and a Republican youth club. No beer, no dope, no cursing. And yet there was a funky, loose and even 'hip' ambiance, partly, it was true, due to the headbands, beads and ponytails but also because of the unstructured way it all worked. Nobody gave orders. Nobody seemed to be in charge. Nobody told anybody to cook, somebody just did it, and Red washed the dishes without being asked.

After dinner he sat down next to me and I said how strange it was that I should feel so comfortable despite being ignored. He said he had noticed the same thing at first. He pointed out a short, thin, serious young man in a khaki army shirt decorated with Indian embroidery . . . *Ateronhiatakon*, which means 'Exploding Sky' and whether by design or accident it had been he who first approached Red.

Red was lying on his bunk, having just finished his first day of painting. Nobody had told him what needed painting or what colour to paint it so he went out on his own, bought some paint and started on the porch. Ateronhiatakon came in and sat on Red's bunk, said he like the colour and asked if he had ever painted before. 'A little,' Red said. Ateronhiatakon asked what work he had done. Red hemmed and hawed and then decided to admit that he had spent most of his life avoiding work.

Ateronhiatakon said: 'When I left high school I had already decided the forty-hour week was not for me. The Indian way was what I wanted, being close to the land, in harmony with nature. The way that is not taught in American books. Most of my friends work off the reservation, in high-rise steel construction. They think their way is better, the American way of industrial progress and all that . . . '

The traditional Indian attitude towards work is such that a person will say, well, we need 800 dollars to get through the winter and he will go out and find 800 dollars' worth of work. Then he quits because that is all he needs for the winter. Indian tradition does not include the accumulation of money. The white man says that Indians are lazy.

Mohawks are known for their ability to balance themselves

105

on high iron. It is highly paid work and many who leave the reservation leave for this reason. Anthropologists have come up with various explanations for this skill, like centuries of balancing on logs down rivers, but bridges were being built across the St Lawrence River in the late nineteenth century and it was practical proximity which gave birth to the skill more than anything else. They get trapped in city finances following high-iron work, financing cars and major appliances, and since Mohawks do not have experience in that situation they are easily exploited. Indians in the city are sad like Gypsies away from their caravans. Indians drink in the city.

'. . . I will not recommend that way to my child,' said Ateronhiatakon. 'I have not even given him an American name, only a Mohawk name. That is all he needs. Indian names are the right names for Indians. We must keep what is ours. They have even given our reservation a white name, the name of a Christian saint, St Regis, while the Indian name is Akwesasne, "the land where the partridge drums". It is difficult, you know, because the society outside shows us a lot of shiny things.'

Red decided not to say anything about the hawk. It might sound condescending, like some white man dabbling in Indian folklore. He only said that he supposed one reason he came here was to escape from the shiny things.

Ateronhiatakon said: 'I'll ride in a car because it is unavoidable, but I won't own one. I own a horse. I won't own a television. I've never travelled overseas. You may think it is funny, but I'm not curious about Europe or Africa. I am curious only about how I can help my people, that takes all my time. A couple of years ago I was invited to an environmental conference in Stockholm but I turned it down because I wanted to learn about seeds. I had other commitments. I don't read books. I've never read a book from cover to cover. The earth is the main thing. You must look under your feet, for me that is a very spiritual thing to do. Mother earth has got to be protected. Maybe I could learn about it from books but I don't want to, I want to go right to the earth. It's going to take my entire life.'

'But you work on the newspaper,' Red said. 'You work with

words.'

'We have talked about that problem many evenings. What should we keep from the white culture? Should we take the best from it and rule the rest out, or reject it all? There are some things I can't ignore, every time I turn around they are there. It's almost insane not to take advantage of them. Like a shovel, that's not an Indian tool. We can't say no to everything, it's impossible. Even the most traditional Indians use electricity. I'm just going to try, I'm going to try like the dickens to live the Indian values, to go back as far and as completely as possible and if I have a Polaroid camera in my pocket, well . . . what can I say? I live in a trailer; we used to live in longhouses but now I live in a trailer. We've talked about this, and talked and talked, we've talked about the basic idea of putting out a newspaper. Indians used to spread the word between communities with tom-toms, or a runner. Who's going to run now? It's easier to put it on paper. My wife and I finish talking about this here, and then we go home and talk about it some more. We say we guess we can't avoid using some of these things but above all we never want to lose our oneness with the earth. We are going to look to the sun and say thank you to it, we are going to look to the moon and say thank you grandmother moon.'

Once more Red thought of the hawk, and of his redwood trees. He remembered the time when, as a child, he had looked up at a clear star-studded sky and applauded. 'Bravo Lord,' he had said. 'Good show', and he had sat down on the grass and laughed and applauded and applauded. Now he said: 'There are a lot of Americans who are talking about the same things.'

'Yes, there are kids in America who are saying they wish they were Indians, who are also rejecting American values. I'm not into that, the so-called "youth culture". I've never even listened to Bob Dylan. Don't be confused by my long hair. That's not just because everybody else has long hair. To us it has a spiritual meaning. From long hair comes tolerance, respect. Our hair is the creator's seal of approval. It's very good that young people are growing their hair though because now there is more tolerance towards Indians with long hair. The white man doesn't call us "squaw" any more.'

After thousands of years of continual tribal existence on the same continent, the Indians had developed a solid philosophy of life which could be verified by looking out of the window. All contradictions had been worked out of it. Then came the Europeans with a highly cosmopolitan, contradictory culture which, as De Gaulle once said about France, was 'constructed by blows of the sword'. The Indians have always suspected the white man's social structure was inferior to their own. Their scepticism waned, however, as the American dream grew rosier. Now that it has begun to pall, scepticism waxes once more. It seems likely that the Indian was right all the time.

Ateronhiatakon continued: 'We know that purification time is arriving, that nature will have to clean itself. It was taught to us a long time ago, an old prophecy which said that we would stray from our ways, we would take a crooked road, and that someday we would come back. It doesn't say when, just that there will be signs. And we have seen signs. The white man talks about ecology now, but the Indians have always been ecologists. When the white man killed the buffalo it was not good ecology. Only the word did not exist then. We did not need the word to understand it was a bad thing to kill all the buffalo. Now there are people freezing in their houses because of the energy crisis, while we have plenty of wood for our stoves. And they are speaking of world-wide famine. The Indian people were warned about this a long time ago, but we did not take heed in time and we will probably be caught by it too because we have forgotten how to grow food. We also depend on the supermarket. But we are learning again. It may be too late, but we are learning.'

'I would like to learn too,' said Red, 'learn about seeds and herbs and roots.'

Ateronhiatakon laughed. 'An old Indian named Cayote passed through here last month and prophesied that there would be some strange people coming out of the cities . . . '

Ancient Iroquois architecture (Mohawks are an Iroquois tribe) featured long, wooden-frame buildings with related families living in separate apartments which were added on to as children grew up and married. In Mohawk, 'Hotinonsionne' means 'People of the Extended House' and

Mohawks refer to themselves that way. 'Mohawk' is a white man's word.

About 25% of reservation youth are 'progressive', that is, conservative. Ten per cent were raised in the longhouse tradition and stayed there. Another 25% are new longhouse people, first-generation kids coming back in from the Catholic side with the renaissance. Since Indians occupied Alcatraz and Wounded Knee, being American is no longer such a great thing. In the middle, floaters, really not sure what to do, where to be, who they are. Comfortable in neither church nor longhouse, they move around American teenage culture, sort of hippies but not really that either, on the fringes of everything, fitting nowhere.

With the inauguration of the era of 'zero growth', the lack of a 'shared ethical vision' became impossible to ignore. Increasing numbers of Americans found it difficult to defend American values. After the fall of Nixon it became harder still, coming as it did at the end of the traumatic Viet Nam War. The American system is a temporal system based on growth, profits and consumption, based on anything but universal truths and it requires a highly reasoned and devious rationale to defend. Some Indians find to their joy that they no longer have to defend it, it is not their system; as the Welsh and Bretons, for example, find they no longer have to defend the English or French systems. They have something better to defend.

'Say . . . ' Red said to me looking at his watch. 'There is . . . I guess you could call it a social at the longhouse tonight. Let's make it over there.'

We trudged a hundred yards though unploughed snow to a long, old wooden building behind. The air was smoky inside, not from cigarette smoke but from a malfunctioning wood stove, the only heat; a sweet, not unpleasant smell but the smoke made your eyes smart. Three kerosene lamps on the wall gave the only light, a dim and primitive light perfectly suited to the tom-toms four young man were beating in a corner. There were some small oil paintings of old feathered chiefs on the otherwise bare, rough walls which matched the floor and ceiling.

'Is the longhouse like a church?' I asked Red.

'It's more than that. It's a way of life. It's not just some institution like the St Regis church where people go on Sunday morning and that's the end of it. The spiritual and political lives of the longhouse people are woven together so tightly that the chiefs are spiritual and political leaders at the same time. There are now some young Mohawks who come to the longhouse and go to church too. They are on the fence, it's delicate. I don't think they can go on like that. The old Mohawk law says they cannot participate in a foreign government. They forfeit their birthright if they do that. The old laws are recited every five years by the chiefs, and I don't mean the Bureau of Indian Affairs chiefs. They are just Uncle Toms.'

Gradually, in small groups, the others drifted over from Nation House to the longhouse. They began to dance ... laughing, jumping and chasing each other in happy undulating circles to the tom-toms, and suddenly I was back in Brittany ... people linking arms and holding hands and dancing *together* like that. I thought again how symbolic it was that dancers in city discotheques never touch each other, how they often turn their backs on each other. I could not figure out the rhythm here, perhaps it was three threes and a four, I wasn't sure. The chain wound and grew and snaked; a surrealistic multi-coloured snake through the smoke, out of time, out of fashion, almost out of sight. I understood that here too the chain was more important than individual style, that you could not really make a mistake so long as you fulfilled your role as a link ... transmitting energy, love, support.

I grew thirsty from the smoke and the dancing and asked Red if we could get a beer somewhere. He said: 'Yeah. That's a good idea. There is something you should see anyway.'

We walked across the road and down half a mile or so, over an iron bridge to a neon-lit structure surrounded by parked cars with a blinking SCHLITZ sign over the door. There were some twenty people inside, Indians trying to look like Americans. Progressives. They were staring into space, sipping beer without enthusiasm. Only a few were speaking to each other. The conversations were short and from what I could hear not very passionate. Again I thought of Brittany, of the tabac across from the Fest Noz, of the same emptiness, lack of contact, lack of spirit, of the contrast with the Nationists across the road.

Somebody put a quarter in the juke-box . . . Mick Jagger singing:

Angie . . . Angie . . .
Where will it lead to from here . . . ?

Two weeks later I received a letter from Red who said that just after I left, Ateronhiatakon took him to a sweat lodge ceremony. He was the only white man there. This ceremony is religious and usually closed and he was told his being there was exceptional. He felt awed and a little afraid. Before the ceremony began, Ateronhiatakon rose and asked those assembled cross-legged on the floor: 'Who here has had something to do with the hawk?'

Seven
Tot Esperant Godot[1]

'I support the left, though I'm leanin' to the right.' –
Cream

On the corner of the Ramblas and some poor alley the
Provincial bought me a raisin-filled drink so strong it ought to
be illegal. We gulped and chewed with the small group there,
a working-class group squashed and boozing under the double
burden of fascism and the church. Waiting for Franco to die.

The Provincial pointed to the only oak on the Ramblas, the
only oak in Barcelona, as a matter of fact, and was proud to
know its location. He was not proud to be a provincial in what
should be a capital. He thought, who is this expert come to
examine my occupation?

Catalonia does not exist. Only four provinces of north-east
Spain, plus the Balearic Islands. There is no minister for
Catalan Affairs. There is no Catalan police department,
Catalan is not taught in the schools. There is no Catalan
railroad, no Catalan Department of Health and not one
Catalan holds a post of any importance in the occupying
(Spanish) government.

'How can there be Catalan anarchists if there is no
Catalonia?' I was remembering the recent news item:

POLICE REPORT BREAKUP OF
CATALAN ANARCHIST GROUP
The breakup of a major anarchist urban guerilla
movement, with three arrests and the seizure of a cache
of arms, explosives and communications equipment was
announced yesterday by Barcelona police . . .

The Provincial thought, who is this good white man come to
study the poor Indians? I'll do a war dance for him: 'I don't

give a shit about politics,' he said. Then he thought, is that old bastard ever going to die?

Catalonia was occupied by the Romans, the Goths and then the Moors. Charlemagne chased out the Moors in 788. Count Raymond Berenger IV of Barcelona married Petronilla of Aragon which annexed Catalonia to Aragon. Queen Isabella of Castile married King Ferdinand of Aragon which annexed Aragon to Castile. Catalonia retained its own government, institutions, its own money, its own ambassadors. Catalonia minded its own business while Castile conquered America . . . grew rich trading in Sicilian wheat in which it had a monopoly. While Castile plundered the Americas, the Catalans remained the Swiss of the peninsula, keeping their sanity and making profits while everybody else went crazy killing people. That is why America speaks Spanish, not Catalan.

In 1640 Catalonia turned to Louis XIII of France to save itself from the occupation of Philip IV of Spain. It turned back to Spain in 1659 and back to France again in 1694. The war of the Spanish succession made Catalonia Spanish for good, though it reverted to France from 1808-13 then back again to Spain. It can be said that the current occupation of Catalonia began on September 11th, 1714, when Philip V formally deprived it of a parliament. With its history of doing business in peace, Catalonia adapted quickly and easily to the Industrial Revolution, providing the industrial product to support the Castilian Army in America. While Castile lost men through wars and emigration, drained itself through long expensive campaigns a continent away, Catalonia grew populous, rich, peaceful. In 1860, when the Castilian Government tried to draft Catalonian men in their army for the first time, there were riots on the streets of Barcelona.

Regarding the bustling night life on the Ramblas, I remembered George Orwell's description of Barcelona (in *Homage to Catalonia*) when it was the capital of an autonomous republic for six years in the 'thirties.

Red flags and red-and-black anarchist flags everywhere. Shops and cafés collectivized. Even boot-blacks collectivized, their boxes painted red and black. Churches gutted. Everyone calling everyone 'comrade' or 'thou'. Tipping forbidden by

113

law, waiters looking you in the face as equals. Private motor cars collectivized, trams painted red and black:

> . . . Down the Ramblas, the wide central artery of the town where crowds of people streamed constantly to and fro, the loudspeakers were bellowing revolutionary songs all day and far into the night. And it was the aspect of the crowds that was the queerest thing of all. In outward appearance it was a town in which the wealthy classes had practically ceased to exist. Except for a small number of women and foreigners there were no 'well-dressed' people at all. Practically everyone wore rough working-class clothes, or blue overalls, or some variant of the militia uniform. All this was queer and moving. There was much in it that I did not understand, in some ways I did not even like it, but I recognized it immediately as a state of affairs worth fighting for . . .[2]

Thin as the miler he was, out of shape now for his thirty-two years, a heavy smoker, pale, the Provincial has a broad smile reminiscent of Gene Kelly but which, despite its breadth, remains ironic . . . a smile in other words, despite there not being enough to smile about. Yes, he too has read *Homage to Catalonia* and, ordering another round, he smiled remembering that state of affairs.

What a mess! Short, tumultuous, tragic . . . what a grand mess. He thought about the revolutionary village committee which, when talked out of killing a priest they had been hunting down for hours, shook hands with each other and with the priest, pleased at the decision. He remembered that at one time the top two men in the revolutionary government of the province of Lérida were chimney sweeps. But that was all before . . .

That state of affairs had long gone. Even the street names were lost, most of them now being named after Franco's friends, allies and generals. Streets now jammed with the so-called 'Spanish Miracle', with honking home-made Fiats and Morrises. While waiters, who, like the rest of the working class, are not allowed unions, look you in the eye not as equals but potential marks.

For the Spanish Miracle, like the Italian Miracle before it, had to do with nothing but money and while it too would soon stall in a mire of unrestrained industrialism, moral torpor and lack of a shared ethical vision, for the moment unrestrained industrialism reigned, making a sooty hell even out of the Sculptor's paradise in the suburbs.

The Sculptor remembers the worms in chocolate when he was lucky enough to get chocolate, when grass soup and cat meat were daily fare. He remembers this in his remodelled sixteenth-century house with the swimming pool on the roof. Those memories are never far from his mind and he is not soon likely to take eating for granted. So he says to his German gallery man: 'What's selling these days? What should I make next?' The German, puzzled, not expecting such pliancy from his stable: 'But . . . *you're* the sculptor.' The Sculptor smiles: 'Yes, and *you're* the salesman.' He is not waiting for Franco to die. He knows he had better make all he can while he can just in case the old man should turn out to be mortal after all.

Sitting and sipping by the Sculptor's pool, the Monarchist laughed at the gallery man. Catalans can teach Germans something about making money. The Monarchist was prepared to wait. Sitting and sipping, the Monarchist by the pool . . . grey hair, brown skin, dandy goatie. He would just as soon everything go on like it is for a while . . . oh, perhaps a bit more liberal here and there, certainly liberal enough to do business with Brussels, but he was realistic enough to be afraid. He knew that the only way to avoid anarchy after Franco was a restoration, a liberal, perhaps even socialist restoration – what's the difference so long as business as usual. Or preferably better than usual. He had just returned from Portugal, where he talked to the Socialist Minister Mario Soares, preparing the ground, and, though he would not like it advertised, he had even met Sanitago Carrillo, the chief Spanish Communist, in Geneva. He too is haunted by memories of wormy chocolate and cat meat.

Turning my back to the sun, I asked the Monarchist why the Provincial drinks. The Monarchist waved a hand in a generous gesture: 'He has a rich wife. I should have his bank account. No need to worry about him.' Sixteen generations

Catalan, the Monarchist can discuss business and politics in perspective, sipping by the pool, with class. The only way to discuss anything: 'Once we get in the Common Market, as we move towards economic and maybe political union with Europe, the Catalan problem will disappear. Because this spirit of nationality in the narrow sense will disappear. Whether we like it or not, small nations cannot survive in the modern world. We can talk about social freedom, the freedom to speak a language and so on, but a monarchy would give that right, that is not much, a language like Catalan spoken by seven million people should have a legal status. But I believe that in a real geo-political sense these little nations are through. And whatever they try to do to save their culture will not be enough. No, one must be firm because once you start giving them autonomy on any level they will end up demanding their political independence as well, and that is clearly unacceptable. What we need is not decentralization but more efficiency at the centre. We in Spain have had too recent a brush with anarchy to let that happen.'

The Provincial and I were by now pushing our way through the midnight mobs in the alleys off the Ramblas: 'After Franco,' I asked, 'will being Catalan become more important than being, say, Communist?'

'It doesn't interest me at all. I think that the current investment in national minorities on the part of the left is only a matter of being à la mode. I'm not interested in selling my soul. To anybody. I just don't give a shit. All those parties are the same . . . nationalist, leftist, whatever. They will never evolve.'

The Provincial smiled to himself, remembering a speech by Garcia Oliver, the Anarchist Minister of Justice (*sic!*) on January 3rd, 1937:

> Justice must be burning hot, justice must be alive, justice cannot be restricted within the bounds of a profession. It is not that we despise books and lawyers. But the fact is that there were too many lawyers. When relations between men become what they should be there will be no need to steal and kill. For the first time let us admit

here in Spain that the common criminal is not an enemy of society. He is more likely to be a victim of society. Who is there who says he dare not go out and steal if driven to it to feed his children and himself? Do not think that I am making a defence of robbery. But man after all does not proceed from God, but from the cave, from the beast. Justice, I firmly believe, is so subtle a thing that to interpret it one has only need of a heart.[3]

Two Catalan strains side by side. Bourgeois and anarchist: both waiting. Meanwhile . . .

Copper-skinned high-rise banks. A St Laurent boutique. Foxy ladies in the cafés. Italian and Yiddish overheard in a toy shop. Polished tables on wide tile sidewalks . . . a liberated student wearing a blue see-through blouse with a Pepsi emblem covering one nipple: 'Don't ask me about Spain. I'm not Spanish, I'm Catalan. Spaniards are those dirty little uncultivated people who come up here from the flattest, least interesting part of the peninsula. They've got no culture, no . . . I'll say it, no class. This may sound snobbish to you but if you stayed here for a while you'd see what I mean. I feel much closer to the French, if I have to choose a neighbour. We have a long border with France. The Catalan language is much closer to Provençal (Occitan) than it is to Spanish. Our history is as much tied to France as to Spain. Our food, our culture, our sense of humour. We even have the same bullshit, that sense of superiority. I can relate to a Frenchman, but to a Spaniard . . . You know in Switzerland one can be German or French or Italian and still feel Swiss. A Swiss can be proud of being Swiss no matter what his culture. They let each other alone in Switzerland. A Swiss passport is the best thing in the world to have. But a Spanish passport? I mean, it's embarrassing. Wait and see what happens after Franco dies. And the sooner the better . . . '

'How come you're talking to me? You don't know me. I could be a cop.'

'Oh, I don't care any more. You get sick of being cautious. I'm tired of waiting for that old bugger to die.'

In as totally a bi-lingual city as I have ever seen, one of them is totally proscribed: Catalan, a musical romance language of considerable grace and strength. Such strength that in a nation with (like the Basque Country) a 50 per cent Castilian immigrant population, it is still more practical to learn Catalan than Castilian. Second-generation working-class immigrants from Andalusia learn Catalan for upward social mobility. If you want a loan from a bank . . . to sell a product . . . to buy insurance . . . to join the jet set . . . to be a successful painter in Barcelona, learn Catalan, not Castilian. But you must pick it up somehow, it is not taught officially anywhere. [4]

Catalan is banned in meetings and publications of city councils and other official bodies and their employees are forbidden its use. It is banned in the law courts, in civil records, in commerce (for letterheads, shop signs, placards, advertisements or trademarks) and in obituary notices.

On March 2nd, 1974, at 9.40 in the morning, the Catalan anarchist Puig Antich was garrotted (mechanically strangled) for having been a member of the Iberian Liberation Movement, a Catalan anarchist group. He had been accused of being an accomplice in the killing of a policeman and of robbing several banks. His lawyers had objected to numerous irregularities during the trial, and repeatedly pointed out that the origin of the bullets had never been proved, but he was garrotted anyway. Like many young anarchists in Barcelona, Antich was a product of the 'Spanish Miracle', bourgeois, and the mass of the clandestine left did not support him for this reason. He was considered something of a dilettante. Some degree of solidarity was achieved by the fact that the executioner was imported from somewhere in the middle of the peninsula, obviously a deliberate insult. Antich's father came to the offices of the Castilian daily *La Vanguardia* to ask that his son's obituary be printed in Catalan. It was.

Some professors teach in Catalan – often at the insistence of their pupils – but they can be and are fired for it. The resistance is generally much less visible and certainly less violent than in the Basque Country. This is because the Catalans are the one Nationist movement in Europe whose language is not dying, whose culture is a majority culture at home. They have Barcelona, a capital. Barcelona speaks Catalan. If Marseille had elected to speak Occitan instead of

French, Occitania would not be such a joke. The Catalans figure time is on their side. And numbers. There are clandestine labour unions and nationalist meetings, but the aim is to maintain the culture for the time when political action will be useful and not suicidal. Besides, military action is not in the Catalan tradition. Neutrality is a Catalan tradition, and reconciliation. Anti-communism among the Catalan right wing is not nearly so strong as in Spain, or in France. The Catalonians feel themselves very much Catalans and they feel strong enough to be able to bide their time.

The culture has been under some degree of proscription for over two centuries. Its literature has survived wave after wave of immigration. Ramón Llull (1233-1316) was the first Catalan writer to break with the Provençal literary tradition of the troubadours. With allegorical novels like the *Book of the Lover* he was the first writer in any Romance vernacular to apply his language systematically to every branch of medieval learning. The fifteenth-century Catalan poet Ausias March would be recognized as one of Europe's greatest had he written in the language of an occupier.

With the confirmation of Spanish occupation in 1714, Castilian was imposed on Catalan schools. Over the course of the next century it appeared as though Castilian had won, as though Catalan would go the way of Occitan, would become a patois for the farm and the café. The eighteenth-century tendency to universalize everything provided an irresistible momentum towards a common language. Ethnics were then 'out'. However, the romanticism of the nineteenth century reversed the tendency, brought a rebirth of 'charming' old languages. In Catalonia, the movement was stronger than the Félibrige in Occitania . . . or rather, it was weaker in itself but stronger in its context because Catalan was a big-city language, at home in Barcelona, while Occitan was already lost in the mountains of southern France, or rattling around a few salons of Paris. Catalan was still the language of the bourgeoisie. The Barcelona bourgeoisie chose Catalan as their language of culture and business in the nineteenth century; it became a mark of class. Supervisory personnel speaks Catalan, unskilled labour speaks Castilian. If a taxi driver owns his own taxi he speaks Catalan, Castilian if he drives for somebody else. One learns to make these distinctions in Barcelona: Spain . . . occupied Catalonia.

Catalonia, seat of the only anarchist government the world has ever known, has produced Dali, Miro, Casals, Gaudi, Picasso. They are Catalan (Picasso by adoption) not Spanish. The catalogue of books currently in print in the Catalan language is one inch thick, 5,192 titles, an eclectic list including, at random, the following:

La Mística de la Feminitat: Betty Frieden
Diari d'un Rector de Poble: Georges Bernanos
El Mite de Sísif: Albert Camus
Funerals a Berlin: Len Deighton
Espàrtac: Howard Fast
Assassinat a La Catedral: T. S. Eliot
Rèquiem Per a Una Monja: William Faulkner
Els Pòtols Místics: Jack Kerouac
El Vell i La Mar: Ernest Hemingway
Qui Mana: Mickey Spillane
Poética Constitucio d'Atenes: Aristotle
Stalin: Una Biografia Política: Isaac Deutscher
Homenatge a Catalunya: George Orwell.

But Catalan is limited by effective censorship to what can be called 'intellectual' matters, the definition of which has been broadened lately to include *Peanuts*, in book form only. There is no daily paper in Catalan, despite the most conservative estimate that five million people speak the language. *Kung Fu* is transmitted in Spanish, not Catalan. There are no Catalan comic strips. The 'common man' will not find his local scandal sheet in Catalan. Catalonia does not exist.

The Provincial has taken me to a dive called the 'Bohemian Bodega', across the stage of which parades a sequence of old, fat, ugly, untalented talent. The audience – mostly young, with a sprinkling of homosexuals – has come to laugh at this kitsch, and there are remarks shouted to the stage which, if not exactly insulting, do not imply respect. Yet the performers stamp their feet, snap veined fingers, blink painted eyelids and smile through more gap than teeth as though topping a bill in

Vegas. The Provincial comes here regularly, it is perfectly surreal for his taste. He shouts remarks too, though with more sympathy, and he also stamps and claps along. He sees these 'losers' on stage prevailing over their losses much as mother Catalonia has prevailed over hers. Catalonia . . . for centuries overrun, occupied, bounced between States, maintaining her dignity while quite literally wiped off the map. Catalonia . . . seat of contradictions . . . a loser with style, with class. Killing time waiting for the next round: 'Two more double Fundadors please . . .'

Why does the Provincial drink so much? Perhaps because he is an anarchist with a rich wife. Or a nationalist without a nation. Or a provincial in what should be a capital. Perhaps because he is just killing time. 'What is there in the Catalan character to produce an anarchist tradition?' I asked him.

The Provincial was by now resigned. Much as he despises the transmission of what passes for 'information', he and I had agreed on many things . . . Gaudi, Orwell, the advisability of anarchism. So over still another round in still another saloon, he answers straight: 'Perhaps it is because we have been denied a government of our own for so long. We have never had the chance to develop a ruling class, any such talent has no place to go. And we are not a bunch of country bumpkins, you know. This is Barcelona!'

'What about snobbism? It's well known how Catalans consider themselves superior to just about everybody. Some people even call them racists . . .'

'Where did you hear that? It's just not true. It's absurd. When the Jews were expelled from Spain they were not expelled from Catalonia. We have absorbed wave after wave of immigrants . . . Jews, Andalusians, Frenchmen, Galicians, Phoenicians . . . my God. We are such a mêlange, we absorb everything here. We can have no illusions about racial purity. Who told you that anyway?'

No matter. I did not argue. The following evening, I was dining with the Ethnic, a Catalan with a dandy flower in the lapel of a velour suit and a cultured purse of the lips. I had met him at the University of Occitania, and the Ethnic had since been to the University of Catalonia in Perpignan and to the Interceltic Congress in Mur-de-Bretagne. He speaks Occitan,

Breton and Catalan and made it clear that he spoke Castilian only out of necessity. He preferred pure languages, he had been telling me. He spoke of nationalism as a cultural necessity in these vulgar times. When the bill came he grabbed it. I pleaded for it, or at least for my share. The Ethnic pounded the table: 'I insist! You are my guest in Catalonia. What do you think we are here . . . a bunch of *Jews.*"

At that moment, the Provincial was settling down at his usual table of the Café del Opera, on the wide and shady promenade of the Ramblas. Starting his nightly rounds, researching the surreal, he ordered his second Fundador of the evening . . . a double. He spread open the evening paper He thought; when is that old son of a bitch ever going to die?

Eight
Same[1]

'. . . to have against you Franco, or Hitler, is one thing, but to have Actinium, Argon, Beryllium, Dysprosium, Palladium, Praseodymium . . . Ruthenium, Samarium, Silicon, Tantalum, Tellurium, Terbium, Thorium . . . Thulium, Titanium, Uranium, Vanadium, Virginium, Xenon, Ytterbium, Yttrium, Zirconium, to say nothing of Europeum and Germanium – ahip! – and Columbium – against you, and all the others, is another . . .' – Malcolm Lowry: *Under the Volcano*

The polar night lasts eight weeks, during which the sun does not rise above the horizon. Snow falls in mid-October and covers the ground until May. Mid-winter temperatures regularly sink to $-14°$ Fahrenheit. Lakes are iced over for eight months. The average layer of snow reaches two feet in the forests and deeper still above the tree line. In the summer the sun does not set for ten weeks and there is continuous light for fifteen.

Now at the end of August the sun hangs just over the horizon at 5 in the afternoon. It has never risen much higher all day. At 6 it is almost in the same place. At 7.30 it begins to sink reluctantly from view but the sky is still traced with blue at ten. For some reason nobody has been able to explain to me the moon moves across the horizon so fast you turn following it . . . moves as through trick photography or in an animated cartoon, and at 3.30 in the morning the sun streams through the window again. If not on another planet, we are at least at the end of this one. There is not too much further to go before we slide over the top and down on the other side.

The weather is paramount in Lappland. It controls politics, sociology, art and economics. Geography runs a close second. The southern border of Lappland is roughly the arctic circle (though there are remnants further south). Finnmark, a Norwegian finger sweeping over Sweden and Finland east to the Russian frontier, is 1,300 miles north of Stockholm, which in turn is another 1,300 north of Marseille, from which I have flown . . . almost as far as across America.

The Lapps combine the reticence of Scandinavians with the *méfiance* of remote mountain people. Although there has been a post-war emergence of Lappish national spirit, a movement to liberate the Lapps from their stigma of inferiority, the movement must be considered secondary to the climate and geography. Demonstrating is uncomfortable in −14° on two feet of snow, and not really terribly useful when there are only reindeer around. Also, this is tolerant Scandinavia, and while a State is a State . . . still, there are States and States. The 'oppression' of the Lapps bears comparison in kind but not degree to that of the Basques, the Catalans or even the Welsh. This is a soft occupation.

Estimates of the Lappish population run from 30,000 to 200,000 depending on the definition of a Lapp. My own estimate is 100,000, based on those who speak the language, or whose parents or grandparents spoke it. That is not necessarily the number who would admit to it. In any case official State estimates run closer to the lower number because officially only a reindeer breeder is counted as a Lapp . . . There are still many, mostly over forty, who prefer to be known as Norwegians, Swedes or Finns. The Lappish population is approximately 60% Norwegian, 30% Swedish, 10% Finnish, with only a fraction of a percent – less than a thousand people – remaining on the Kola Peninsula of the U.S.S.R.

First, however, back down 'south' to sombre Uppsala, six Swedish miles (66 kilometres) from Stockholm, home of a university founded in 1477, where we find Israel Ruong, ex-chairman of the National Union of Swedish Lapps, member of the Nordic Lapp Council, editor of *Same Idag*, a Lappish magazine, writer, translator, linguist, professor of Lappish.

'Where does the "Israel" come from?'

'My mother was quite influenced by the bible. Ruong is a Lappish name. I was eight before I could speak a word of Swedish. But I loved to read. I read and read and I went to college. I became a teacher and began to study psychology here in the south.'

A heavily lined face in a double-glazed room. Behind, an August autumn blows orange leaves noiselessly from the trees. The first heat of the season hisses from the radiator. Lovely deep-set eyes, tossed grey-grey hair, a whiff of muted winter in a picture window. Reference books propped open on reading racks, and strewn about. Another wilderness winter missed in the winter of old age.

'Have you lived in Uppsala a long time?'

An Oriental flavour in the Occident, more specifically Eskimo, in any event not particularly Swedish: 'Yes . . . long. But I go back to the wilderness whenever possible.' Something tinkles.

'Do you miss the wilderness?'

'Yes, I miss the seasons. One does not feel the seasons here in the south. I miss that feeling of rebirth when the sun first appears over the horizon before the spring-winter. I miss the violent colours of the foliage at this time of year. I miss the space. But I saw that my people needed me and I began to collect material on Lappish culture a long time ago, to preserve it. That is what I see as my task.'

'Is the Lappish language dying?' The tinkling again, more persistent this time, like icy wind-chimes.

'Yes. Oh . . . I used to be very pessimistic, but no longer. When I see the young people now. The young people have changed so.'

'What has made them change?'

'You ask what? You mean why now? Education. Media. Contact with the outside world. They find they do not like the world so much. Now there is a Nordic Lapp Institute in Kautokeino Norway, run by the young people; this has been my dream for so long, from the beginning, from the first Internordic Conference of 1953 . . . yes, a human being cannot be anything of value unless he has some direct contact with his cultural heritage. That is like a tree without roots. There is a poem by a Lappish poet, Paulus Utsi:

> . . . The wounds in the root
> are not quickly healed.
> But it is happy

when the wind tests the shoots.
Self-confidence now rises
and faith that their generative power
will carry on the heritage.

'But why now? There is a reversal, a reaction to cultural uniformity. The Swedes today must be made to understand that it is to their advantage to help Lappish culture. A multi-cultural State is a healthy State. The young people now are doing this, they are very active now. They see what conformity has done to the human spirit, deprived it of its uniqueness. I am so happy about the new attitude of the young Lappish people.'

'I was advised to call your people *Same,* not Lapps.'

'Oh for me a name is not important. Lapp comes from the Finnish word for wilderness. The young nationalists feel we should be called *Same* not Lapps, we should have our own name. It is important to the young people.'

'Is that something like the difference between Negro and Black in America?'

'Yes, yes. That's it. There was an American ambassador here, a Mr Holland, he was a Negro. When there were demonstrations against the war in Viet Nam, some black Americans here called him a House Nigger.'

'I suppose there are some House Lapps too?'

'I have always found that the best way is from the inside. Slowly, slowly . . . to get the right ideas across to the authorities. It has always seemed to me to be my task to convey the cognitive framework that is uniquely Lappish to the Swedes, that I should be the link between these people. You see authorities, bureaucrats . . . their thinking is so stiff and narrow, I have struggled so much to change the thinking of bureaucrats. But young people today are more impatient. Maybe my methods are no longer so good. Maybe times have changed. I think many of the young Lapps are calling *me* a House Lapp . . . '

I call them Lapps not *Same* because that is how the world knows them and like the Gypsies that is how even the most militant *Same* often refer to themselves. There are several theories as to their origins. One that they migrated from Asia. The other, which Israel Ruong supports, has them inhabiting Finnmark since the Ice Age. The coastal strip was seasonally free from ice then, human beings could have lived there and archaeologists have found artifacts up there dating from the Stone Age, dwellings 6,000 years old. Whichever is the case, the Lapps moved south as the Celts moved west.

There is historical evidence that Lapps were in southern Finland in the fourteenth century. There are Lappish place-names around the Gulf of Bosnia; for example, Lappeenranta (Lapp Inlet) very near Helsinki. Then, just as the white man pushed the North American Indian west, the Lapps were pushed back north by the Scandinavians.

They were settled hunters and fishermen. Reindeer farming was only another 'crop'. Their famed nomad existence is recent; moving with the reindeer herds to the coast or the mountains in the summer, back to the forests in the winter . . . from forty to fifty Swedish miles from summer to winter. The Lapps are mentioned by the Roman historian Tacitus during the first century A.D.[2] He calls them 'Fenni', Finn. Thus Finnmark, 'Lapp territory'. The Vikings raided and traded with the Lapps for furs, a trade gradually cornered by the Finns, who formed 'Bicarls', or trading companies for that purpose. King Gustav Vasa of Sweden was the first to claim the Lappish wilderness as State territory in 1544, just twelve years after the union of Brittany with France, and eight years after that of Wales with England. 'The Lappish wilderness', he said, 'belongs to God and the Swedish Crown and none other.'

The first missionaries arrived. The fur trade attracted Swedes, Danes, Norwegians and Russians, who competed with the Bicarls. Gustav Vasa's son, Charles IX, proclaimed himself 'King of the Lapps in the northern lands'. The first homesteaders arrived.

With them came fences and liquor. Silver was discovered in the mountains. More missionaries arrived. Frontiers shifted after northern wars. The treaty of 1751 fixed the Swedish-Norwegian frontier more or less permanently. Attached to the treaty was a rider which allowed the Lapps to move freely from State to State with their reindeer, and to use the land and water of both Sweden and Norway as subsistence for themselves and their animals 'for ever in peace and war'.

Land acts of 1863, 1864, 1876, 1895 and 1902 confirmed the rights of the reindeer breeders. Thus the Lapps became a sort of guild rather than a national minority: the only laws relating to the Lapps specifically involve reindeer-breeding and related activities. Now as reindeer-breeding becomes an industry with helicopter herding concentrated in fewer families, the definition assumes less and less meaning. It tends to divide the Lapps among themselves, giving a decreasing minority recognition and advantages the majority (both Lappish and Scandinavian) is jealous of.

The land act of 1902, still in force, forbade the sale of land to private persons if it would interfere with the migratory routes of the Lapps, or even if it could be foreseen that it would some day interfere with them. Inexorably, however, as land ran out in the south, as technology tamed the harsh climate, as mineral deposits were discovered, the Lapps were pushed back.

Still more missionaries arrived. Lars Levi Laestadius converted the Lapps in the eighteenth century, a hard conversion, a reaction to the heavy drinking and 'loose morals' he found there. The early Laestadians were not allowed to dance, to sing their ancient chants (*yoiks*) or even to hang curtains on their windows. Lappish religion had been Shamanistic, with a holy man trained to influence the spirits, a religion based on nature with thunder gods, sun gods, and so on. When a person became ill it was thought to be because his soul had left him temporarily and a shaman was the only one who knew how to bring it back. The shamans' knowledge included astronomy, history and anatomy and it was handed down orally. There is to this day no written history of the Lapps. The missionaries brought their own history with them.

Lappish is a Finno-Ugrian language, a division of the Ural-Altaic family which includes Hungarian, Estonian and Finnish. There are three main dialects. Southern Lappish is just about finished, only some hundreds speak it. The Finnish dialect is not in much better shape. The middle dialect spoken in Norway and northern Sweden has the best chance of surviving. It is taught in Norwegian schools until the fourth grade, regarded as an aid to teach Lappish children Norwegian. About 30% of the Norwegian Lapps speak no Norwegian and do not, for instance, understand what happens to them in the courts.

Lappland is booming. Like most booms in the Fourth World, the economic benefits are not felt so much there as in the centre. Iron, copper, nickel and chrome have been discovered in large quantities, much of it still unexploited. Many Lapps now work in the mines and while it is true such work is very well paid, it is also true that the operation is run for the good of the south.

The ever-increasing need for energy has caused an explosion of hydro-electric projects. Networks of high-tension wires invade the wilderness. Canals and dams block the reindeer. Roads feeding mines block the reindeer. Production-line forestry destroys traditional winter feeding grounds by burying winter food – Lichen moss – under the detritus. Tourist stations multiply to service ever larger numbers of campers, hikers, hunters and fishermen. Like the Indians, the Lapps have seen their land gobbled up in bits and pieces for 'the good of the State'.

The third most important element in Lappland – after climate and location – is its low population density. Whether or not we include the Kola Peninsula, Lappland is still bigger than England, with a total population, Lapps plus everybody else, of less than a million. The fourth element is ecology. Only then comes politics. Lappish politics are tied to those first four elements more than to any other political elements in the world down there. This is a wilderness where the sun does not rise or set on schedule and where the moon spins like a top around the horizon, the last wilderness in Europe.

Kiruna, Swedish Lappland, a modern miracle in the wild north, faces its mountain of iron ore like a jousting knight . . . armed, poised, rearing. Jackhammers, bulldozers and climbing cranes. Birds squawk in wide, erratic circles, fish dive for cover, reindeer run in fear towards a forest which no longer exists. Wide streets with smart houses set back from them in unabashed imitation California. High-rises, modern hotels, Diners' Club, freezers for sale, colour TV in the lobby, Volvos. The one cinema in town is featuring *Memories Within Miss Aggie,* American porn à la Ingmar Bergman, the perfect image for Kiruna.

The largest town in the world, 20,000 square kilometres, the entire north of Sweden. Bigger than L.A. they tell you proudly. Jets up from Stockholm are jammed Sunday night and Monday morning, back down again Friday night and Saturday morning. Something like Brasilia, a place to live in the future maybe, not now. Mines, marshalling yards, The European Space Research Organization rocket launching facility on the Vittangi River, a glacial research station at Tarfala Lake, close by Kebnekaise Mountain (at 2,117 metres the highest mountain in Sweden) all within the city limits. A population of 222 in 1900, 11,000 in 1948 when the first town charter was drawn, 40,000 now. Private planes and snow scooters (motorized sleds) are common. Recently inaccessible mountains and lakes have beer cans on them. The Swedish Army Commando School has arrived. The Lapps say, stay out of the wilderness, it is ours 'for ever, in peace and in war'. Kirunians answer, this is a socialist State. Everybody should be able to enjoy the wilderness. It's not your private property. The Lapps say, feebler and feebler, our reindeer can no longer calve, our herds are dying, it is our living, our way of . . . life . . .

The traffic system of Kiruna is so set up that all streets in the *centrum* are dead-end and so whatever through traffic there is misses it. You can walk in the middle of the streets in the *centrum.* A teenage boy ski-poles on roller skates in the middle of the *centrum.* Two elderly ladies drink Coca Cola in the middle of the street. A young Lapp limps along in his blue and red embroidery, climbs into a steel-grey Mercedes and honks at the two ladies backing up. I pass a candy store where some hard-core porn catches my eye. I wait to pay for it behind a three-year-old girl buying 35 cents' worth of gum drops. This is *Swedish* Lappland, a morality the Lapps are not particularly pleased to be occupied by.

Swedish radio broadcasts some international Lappish news in Lappish each day: ' . . . The Finnish Lapp organization is working against the plan to outlaw hunting wolves in Finland . . . '

Ecology takes funny twists in Lappland. The wolf was once a forest animal, now it has been chased north by civilization to the mountains. Similarly you never saw a lynx up here a generation ago. The law protects these animals with the best ecological intention, but the ecology has been disrupted 500 kilometres south and the animals are being pushed north just as the Lapps once were. Now the Lapps must spend half their time protecting their reindeer from the wolves and the lynxes. They say, if you don't allow us to kill them, keep them out of here. The Scandinavians say, if we allow you to kill them we must allow everybody to kill them and then there will be too many killed. The Lapps say, just let *us* kill them. The Scandinavians say, that is not democratic.

Scandinavians say that hydro-electric power is good ecology and who cares about a few reindeer anyway. They say the world needs paper and the only way to get it and keep it reasonably priced is through mass-production forestry, and this too is good ecology and who cares about a few reindeer anyway. The Lapps, then, are put in the position of standing in the way of progress, which maybe they are. Hydro-electric power is not destructive progress and, indeed, who cares about a few reindeer?

BUT IT'S MY LAND!!! YOU KEEP TAKING MY LAND AND YOU DON'T PAY ME FOR IT!!!!!

No, that is misleading. It should not be in caps and with exclamation points. The Lapps say it very softly, they make no trouble about it, they retreat softly in the snow with tinkling herds, they go to work in the mines, they service tourists.

'Although we are good Swedish citizens, our people feel certain pressures in this society which make them ashamed to be Lapp. People ask why we should be able to hunt and fish in the mountains while they can't. They do not understand why we want to learn our mother tongue in school. They will never understand how we can feel more Lappish than Swedish . . . ' Maj-Lis Skaltje, a producer for the Lappish section of Swedish radio. She has a sweet, clear voice like falling snow and a tinkling laugh which reminds me of the wind-chimes back in Israel Ruong's study, and of the busload of Swedish tourists in the Ferrum Hotel last night.

I had walked in there hoping for dinner but found the dining room taken by eighty prim people propped sternly at lined tables all with little glasses of pink wine in front of them. It took me a few minutes to realize what was wrong. It was a scene without sound. Somebody had forgotten to run the soundtrack. Eighty people on holiday and there was no sound. Just a tinkling like some northern wild-track, a filtered sound as though softened by snow though it was still summer. No noise, no speech, no toasts, just the tinkling of pink wine and silver and even that din as though floating in from some other movie like those wind-chimes, like Maj-Lis Skaltje's laugh . . .

' . . . What's so special about Lappish culture?' they ask. 'Isn't ours good enough for you?' They are insulted somehow. They consider us old-fashioned and bad socialists when we insist on staying in our little isolated villages where we feel safe and happy with our families rather than coming into the cities. They must maintain water and electricity and other services for only a small number of people in these villages, which is inefficient and shows we lack 'communal' spirit. They say, 'All right, we can't force you to move into Kiruna, but then you won't get your mortgage for a new house . . . '

There is a railway from Kiruna west across the fjords to the port of Narvik, Norway. The city of Kiruna wants a motor road alongside it. The Lapps say the motor road will bring too many tourists roaring around upsetting the reindeer. What do you need a road for, they ask, there's already a railroad? The Swedes say, it is important for miners who are digging under the earth all day to be able to get to nature on weekends. You are not good socialists, the Swedes say.

'I would like a paved road to my village,' said the young Lapp reindeer breeder, 'so I can get my meat to market before it spoils in summertime.'

'Ah I see,' said the councillor. 'Now you *want* roads. I thought you Lapps didn't like roads. So then you have also changed your mind about the road to Narvik?'

'No, I just want a road to my village. I didn't say anything about the road to Narvik.'

'Well, in that case I don't see how I can help you,' said the councillor.

'That's not fair,' said the young Lapp.

South to Jokkmok, a good Macadam road, in a Volkswagen rented from a young blond-bearded hustler whom I had already noticed jamming gears into reverse, squealing around corners, holding an intense conversation with a businessman in the lobby of The Ferrum. People work like crazy in Kiruna, do nothing else but work for two or three years and then take their bundle back down to civilization. Hardship bonuses are generous. And there are some like Nils, the desk clerk in my hotel, who tells me he is here because 'in Stockholm there are a million people and nobody knows anybody while in Kiruna there are only forty thousand and everybody knows everybody.'

The Samernes Folkhögskola (Lappish Community College) in Jokkmok has the folklorique token look of a reservation institution. A bright showcase reservation, a clean place to take the senator. New paint on old surfaces. 'Charming' rather than functional. Rusticity for the rustics. Minor for the minority.

Mrs Ostlund, a sturdy, intelligent, committed Swede born in Lappland, tells me the school was started in the 'forties by missionaries with a good Christian education in mind. Even though there are subsidies from the centre, still she hears the authorities say: 'Sweden has an excellent public school system. Isn't it good enough for you?'

Sitting at a wooden picnic table in an adjoining wood, we are attacked by a bevy of gnats. I have timed my visit to miss the mosquito season. Lappland is the mosquito capital of the world in July and early August. Driven inside, we settle next to piles of books in the director's office, one of which is (in English) Jerome K. Jerome's *Three Men in a Boat*. Mrs Ostlund admits her school is a far cry from what she calls the 'Bantu policy' of the old nomad schools – a policy of teaching the primitives only their place, separate but unequal. There has been progress, but still . . . hers is the only school to teach the history of the Lappish people.

'Does the history of Sweden look different from the Lappish point of view?'

'You know, colonialized people always learn their history

133

backwards.'

'Do you consider the Lapps colonialized? Like the Basques, for example?'

'No, no, not so blatant. There's no official policy of exploitation or oppression here. Just ignorance and neglect. If you want to compare the Lapps with any other national minority, I think there are parallels with the Kurds. Because the problem is of a more or less primitive indigenous nation living on what has become rich land cut by many State borders. A nation being sacrificed through nobody's "fault". But we've got to rethink the whole basic question of welfare in this country. This is very subjective . . . we have had the same government for forty years and it believes there is nothing better than to be a welfare Swede. That is a person with absolutely materialistic values. This county is well off, no doubt, but if you were to stay a while you would see that the people are not happy. They lack something. In my opinion they lack roots. Have you read Israel Ruong's speech about the exploitation of the land and the forests up here? He is one of the leaders . . . '

'He told me that some young militants think of him as a "House Lapp".'

'Yes, I'm afraid I've heard that said about him. Some say that he has only worked to further his career. Personally, I don't agree. He has been a good spokesman. I think it is important that the Lapps have their own spokesmen. Because through history and even nowadays there are always a lot of other people speaking on their behalf. As a minority you are always an object, and one of our problems is that experts from all over the world come up here and they want help and materials for their investigations and so forth and they give nothing back and we are a little tired of it by now. The *Sames* are getting very tired of experts studying them under a microscope, as it were.'

'You mean people like me?'

'Like you.'

The road north to Kautokeino is a paved strip through two hundred miles of absolutely nothing. Thirty miles between gas stations and nothing to the horizon in any direction. Lost and a bit frightened in this unaccustomed space, I think . . . so I have become an 'expert. I remember my only journalistic 'scoop', the 'revolutionary bust' of Timothy Leary by Eldridge Cleaver in Algiers in 1971. Then I became an instant 'expert' on the Black Panthers. One coincidental coup and three articles in the *Village Voice* and presto one more expert. I held command performances of my tapes around London, where I was living at the time, carrying Xerox copies of the articles for reading-along, and an auxiliary speaker for greater tape fidelity. Groups in salons asked me questions. I learned first-hand how the revolutionary star system works.

There are already too many experts running around telling us what we ought to do or not do. How can I convince these people I am no expert? It had taken me many intimate hours to convince the Provincial. I consider experts like States . . . establishments requiring devolution. I must be sure to get across that I am only trying to cope with my occupation through learning about the occupation of others. No, no . . .

Emptiness. Nothing upon nothing. Less than one car every ten minutes. Signs to villages 15 kilometres away with silhouettes of walkers on them, 15 kilometres from the main and only road accessible by vehicle only in winter when the snow scooters once more emerge. Lappland waits for winter, summer in Lappland is the time for hibernation. The leaves now are orange and red and the temperature sinks lower towards frost each day. Life is approaching: when the snow falls, all of this will spring to life; when the tourists and experts leave.

Bad roads in Finland, dinkier houses around the gas stations and alongside the lakes. Big boulders strewn in stagnant pools. The border at Kersuando had been a bright yellow steel barge across a rushing blue river, not much of a border, a gentle and easy border but a demarcation nevertheless between the prosperous State of Sweden and what is obviously the bumpier State of Finland. Two kids kicking a football. A semi-trailer loaded with heavy timber. One Hungarian Volkswagen with luggage piled high on a roof-rack driven by a long-haired youth. A farmer on a bike. Between, nothing under a heavy, windy, hanging sky. Nothing on the only road. Norwegian Immigration is a wooden building huddling beside a drop-pole over the road. Another easy border.

But borders nevertheless. Borders cutting a nation. A natural geographic and cultural entity artificially cut. Natural neighbours and organic activities wedged apart. To telephone from Kiruna, Swedish Lappland, to Kautokeino, Norwegian Lappland – 300 kilometres apart – the connection goes 1,500 kilometres south to Stockholm then across west to Oslo then back up again north-east 1,800 kilometres to Kautokeino. Mail goes the same way. The Kola Peninsula, now Soviet Russia, is an even harsher cut. The thousand or so Lapps living there are totally lost to their nation. One hears of reindeer co-operatives that work well there, but one only hears, one hears little and one hears through the roundabout connection ... down to Moscow, across to Helsinki, Stockholm or Oslo and then back up again.

I am overcome by loneliness remembering Kautokeino, my loneliness there. The expert, unwanted, tired, alien. I read *Under the Volcano* in my hotel room there and the desolation of that tropical tragedy fitted the arctic and my personal desolation, perhaps illogically, but well. I drank Schnapps in Kautokeino, drank to interview, to sleep, to read, to accommodate the isolation of the arctic and an unwelcome image of expert.

Kautokeino, a bend in a river, a shallow valley between nondescript hills, unpaved, a frontier settlement with one overpriced tourist hotel staffed by surly Norwegians. Empty now as the season draws to a close, only some lonely soldiers and miners left to sip joyless beer in the lobby. Wishing they were somewhere else.

The *Sámi Institut'ta* (Lapp Institute), Israel Ruong's dream, less than a year old, is, however, right where it wants to be. It is in these remote wilds on national principle, and to avoid experts like me; people from the centre, collectors of ethnic information and statistics, people who consider this very centre of the Lappish national homeland the 'remote wilds'. There had been disagreement after the three Scandinavian States allotted funds for the Institute. Where to put it? It should be in Tromsø, the States' experts said, part of the university there like any other institute. But the Lapp staff insisted on being at the heart of Lappland, here where the *Same* are still in the majority. Now the Experts in Oslo, Stockholm and Helsinki wonder what the hell is going on up here in the sticks.

My problem is not unlike the early days of a pioneer on Mars. This is not my planet, this planet is not used to visitors and is afraid of invasion. The sun and seasons do not arrive on schedule here. There is absolutely no reason why they should welcome visitors here. Visitors have meant bad news for centuries. Some Lapps murdered a missionary here in Kautokeino a century ago. This is not a place that takes kindly to visitors. Still, understanding this does not lift my freezing gloom. I feel aggression well, I have come so far to find such a reluctant welcome, perhaps it is the Schnapps. I remember that Richard Nixon once said something about never losing his temper except on purpose. Perhaps this is a good time to lose it ... for once I would enter the situation, tired of observing, time to impose myself...

The letter. I must mention the letter. I had written to the Institute a year earlier, upon first learning of its formation. My letter included a clipping of one of my minority articles and asked for information about the Institute and about the Lapps. There was no reply. I wrote a follow-up, also unanswered, and now, having physically entered the place, I asked Per Mikael Utsi about my letters. Utsi, a long-haired Nordic type in his twenties, calls in a secretary to ask about the letter. The institute is full of telephones, electric typewriters, conference tables, steel desks, photo-copying machines and such office finery. It is a well-stocked, funded office resembling, in its surface roughness, in the roughness of the dress of the mostly male staff and in its remote location, the field office of a large and prosperous construction company. The secretary produces my 'file' in something like two minutes. There was the letter, my clip, and a handwritten reply which had never been typed or mailed. The reply demanded that I prove myself, it accused me of being only one more 'expert' coming up here to 'exploit' the Lapps. Who are *you* to bother us, its tone demanded.

Looking around the office with its smooth flow of paper, I see how here I suffer from the lack of a letterhead. They not I

. . . *they* are the experts, *I* am the minority. If my letter had had *Harvard* or *New York Times* on top of it, would it not have been answered? Bureaucracies are designed to deal with other bureaucracies. Doesn't this office have all the hallmarks of a bureaucracy, another 'smoothly' functioning office created to deal with papers rather than people, created to produce a file in two minutes? Like other bureaucracies, dealing with form rather than substance? The substance of this particular matter was certainly to answer my letter, to communicate with someone desirous of opening communication concerning the very substance of this office's work. If one believes, as one is led to believe in Nationist circles, that the devolution of power will lead to a more humane, less impersonal society, here, I thought, is one discouraging example. I decided to lose my temper.

'I'm not the expert,' I growled to Utsi. 'You are. This letter is bullshit!'

Cool, calm, showing no emotion, very Swedish, Utsi answers in a quiet voice with an ironic smile: 'Yes, maybe we are experts. We have to get money from the State, we have to play their game. We don't particularly like playing their game but we have work to do and that is the important thing. You have no idea how many people come up here wasting our time with questions, without any understanding or sympathy for our problems. They don't give anything, they just take.'

Trying to prove I am prepared to give as well as take, I tell him about my moving to Occitania, about my hipster past, my theory of occupation . . . about people I have met in Wales, the Basque Country, about the Mohawks . . . going on for fifteen minutes before realizing that Per Mikael Utsi has been glancing at his watch.

Why do I feel I must prove myself to him? This is just another manifestation of Radical Chic. Coming from the collective guilt of a majority I was not even part of. I used to feel the same way dealing with Blacks in the States, always trying to prove I was good enough for them, I wanted above all to be accepted by them. Blacks could do no wrong. Even if I suspected they did, I repressed such doubts. Whether or not the Black Panthers murdered their enemies in good old totalitarian fashion used to be less important to me than their political aims. I suppressed the subjective in favour of an objective which, it turned out, could not be sustained, and I have since come to believe that even if it could it would be no different in kind from present politics just because of that very suppression. Somewhere we in the American movement lost track of the principle of bettering the *human* condition.

And here in Kautokeino I could not even lose my temper on purpose. This was a minority after all. Poor minority . . . let's not pick on them. And yet if we have learned anything from the failures of the 'sixties, it should be the necessity of criticism, the importance of maintaining the human dimension, the value of confrontation. I wanted to continue confronting Utsi but was afraid to offend a minority, so, as if hearing the words coming from another mouth, I instead form the objective question: 'What sort of work do you do here?'

Utsi sighs, resigned, slides deeper into his chair. He says they are working on a programme to co-ordinate Lappish studies in all the schools of their three Scandinavian sponsors, working to establish a centre for *Same* radio and television programming, to produce the first written history of the Samish people, they will train translators for *Sames* who do not understand Norwegian, Swedish or Finnish. He tells me other things I have already written about. The anger drains, my temper is 'found', I feel the first spots of a migraine. I seem to hear a tinkle again, the lonely icy tinkle of arctic wind-chimes although that may only be the migraine. I interview Aslak Nils Sara, the director of the Institute, like Utsi trained in the universities of the south and now back home with a dedicated air. He too tells me many things I have already written about. He too glances at his watch.

Back in my prefabricated hotel room I finish a pint of Schnapps. Outside it looks like snow. I open *Under the Volcano*. I read:

. . . Not long ago it was poor little defenseless Ethiopia. Before that poor little defenseless Flanders. To say nothing of course of the poor little defenseless Belgian Congo. And tomorrow it will be poor little defenseless Latvia. Or Finland. Or Piddledeedee. Or even Russia. Read history. Go back a thousand years. What is the use of interfering with its worthless, stupid course? . . . What in God's name has all the heroic resistance put up by poor little defenseless peoples all rendered defenseless in the first place for some well-calculated and criminal reason . . . to do with the survival of the human spirit?

Just go back to Tolstoy's day. Then it was poor little defenseless Montenegro. Poor little defenseless Serbia. Or go back a little further still . . . when it was poor little defenseless Greece . . . poor little defenseless Corsica . . .

Why can't people mind their own damned business!

Malcolm Lowry, *Under the Volcano*[3]

Nine
MOB

'The holes in your Swiss cheese are somebody else's
Swiss cheese.' – Melvin Fishman

Minding their own damned business may be all we can hope
for. It may be enough.

'MOB,' William Burroughs called it. 'My Own Business . . .
the right of any individual to possess his inner space, to do
what interests him with people he wants to see . . . On the one
side we have MOBs dedicated to minding their own business,
on the other we have the enemies of MOB dedicated to
interference.'

Good politicians mind their own business, bad ones
interfere. It has nothing to do with left and right. The
Russians were not minding their own business in
Czechoslovakia. The Algerian war ended when France
decided to mind its own business. The Viet Nam War would
never have escalated to such a level had America minded its
own business. MOB is the real issue involved in social
controversies such as birth control, the divorce laws, drug
laws, the abortion controversy. The real issue in these cases
has little to do with the 'issues'. You may, for example, believe
abortion to be a sin against God or nature, that it is immoral
and you are entitled to act accordingly with respect to your
own body. But how can you justify on democratic grounds –
the foundation, after all, of our society – the imposition of that
philosophy on the body of another? That is not minding your
own business.

For centuries we have justified such interference in the very
name of what it destroys. Democracy. Majority rule. Majority
rule, however, is not democratic with units as large as they
have become. The minority has become too large. The
imposition of the preference of 51% on 49% is not democratic

when, as in the case of the French elections of May 1974, 49% is 30 million people, many of whom live 500 miles away from the centre. Forty-nine per cent of the French electorate wanted a socialist system, more than 20% a Communist system. (Whether or not it would have made any difference is something else, the point is they *think* it would make a difference.) Thirty million Frenchmen are now occupied.

The units have become unwieldy. Democracy does not work when there are so many 'losers' ... remote, resentful, occupied by alien values without their consent. The experts say: 'Leave it to us, contemporary society is complicated and nobody is better qualified to cope with it than we technocrats. Give us time. We will make it function.' That is one solution, leave it to the technocrats. However, experts tend to be enemies of MOB, inflicting their expertise on us for our own good whether we like it or not.

There is another solution to the complexities of our time, and that is to reduce the problems to their essence ... to one human, simple, pure common denominator. MOB. Everybody is an expert on the subject of MOB, you need no specialized training, no licence. Leave the experts their proper fields – banking, chemistry, steel, electronics, medicine – but reduce all *human* affairs, that is politics, the structure within which experts must work, to the level of MOB. Is this unrealistic? Idealistic? No ... such a system already exists. We have a model: that admirable collection of MOBs, the Swiss.

What?! The Swiss?! Those small bourgeois minds which have produced nothing but chocolate, Heidi, numbered bank accounts and the cuckoo clock? Are you seriously holding up *Switzerland* as a revolutionary model? Well ... (a little embarrassed) ... yes.

'We would be happy with autonomy on the Swiss model,' Nationists everywhere had told me. I suspected that the model was cited without real understanding, that it was being endowed with a myth it did not deserve, but I have long had a weakness for Switzerland and was pleased to have an excuse to return there 'on business'. I love the softness of small Swiss cities, the feeling one has in that spectacular country of being in a well-lubricated society. It has, in fact, seemed something of a model to me too, also without a real understanding of it.

So, I thought, all right: let's see.

In 1291 three Alpine valleys now known as 'primitive Switzerland' signed a covenant of confederation:

> ... In view of the troubled times, the men of Uri, the moot (a local assembly of freemen) of the valley of Schwyz and the community of the lower valley of Unterwalden have for the better protection and seemly preservation of them and theirs most faithfully vowed to stand by one another with help, advice and all favour, with their lives and worldly goods ... with might and main against all and every man that dare do them all, or any of them ill, either by force, annoyance or injury done or intended to their life and goods ...

The three valleys were tired of being overrun by the Holy Roman Empire and thought they might resist it better together. Other valleys joined the confederation ... Lucerne in 1332, Glarus in 1341, Lug in 1365, the city-states of Zurich and Bern in 1351 and 1353 respectively. More valleys and city-states joined to resist the Hapsburgs. Since they were cut off from each other by snow for the entire winter, they by necessity maintained autonomy over their own affairs, delegating up to the federation only those clearly federal responsibilities which at first were only defence.

Together, by controlling all strategic Alpine passes, the confederation could defend itself merely by thowing down rocks. They stood over the St Gotthard and the St Bernard and the others and threw rocks for centuries. They became fierce warriors. The entire male population of a valley would come out fighting and they fought bravely for and in the company of their own MOB. Experience plus underdevelopment due to the fierce terrain drove the Swiss to export mercenary soldiers who fought in all the armies of Europe including the Pope's (the present Papal Swiss guard is the last remnant of this tradition), Swiss often fighting Swiss. Centuries of fighting took the fight out of them and after more valleys and city-states joined the federation they agreed they had had enough fighting and declared their 'neutrality in the conflicts and wars of all powers, great and small'. The Swiss rejected war as an instrument of national policy. Swiss neutrality is constitutional ... 'perpetual'. Confirming mountain-people instincts, they became, in effect, isolationists.

At the age of ten in the suburbs of New York I had a fist-fight with a kid named McGee who had called me a 'Hebe'. I wasn't going to let him get away with that. McGee beat the shit out of me, shouting 'Hebe' all the while and I decided then and there that fighting would not solve anything, I decided on a policy of perpetual neutrality.

There were doubts and anxieties until I reached the age of sixteen when I discovered my compatriots the hipsters, discovered that I was only being 'hip' and 'cool', because outside of this ethic brave men went out to fight every so often to prove how brave they were. I had been afraid I might be a coward. But as I began to read and become obsessed by music I grew convinced that it took courage to declare perpetual neutrality and that fighting could and must be avoided in all situations other than direct physical attack. Aggression, that pejorative behaviour America has ameliorated – as in an 'aggressive salesman', or an 'aggressive line-backer' – seemed to me something to tame rather than develop. I became an isolationist. I resolved never to involve myself in other people's foreign wars, in foreign aggressiveness. I avoided clubs for this reason and even at the height of the hippy revolution when it seemed as though the world was indeed 'a changin'', I refrained from lending wholehearted support to the legions of Jerry Rubin and Abbie Hoffman. I decided long ago that the most I could expect from my society was to be left alone by it. That was the start of my occupation.

An isolationist in my personal life, I remained a lip-service One-Worlder. Everybody I knew was a One-Worlder. Isolationism was reactionary. These were concepts not to be questioned. But internationalism has become more a euphemism for interference than anything else and it is time to re-examine isolationism in the light of new equations. Nationists are isolationist in the sense that they are concerned with their own problems first, if not exclusively. Nationists are the new radicals. They are against *the* reactionaries, *the* State. It may be then that isolationism is now radical.

Is isolationism merely an excuse for selfishness? To what extent is neutrality a manifestation of cowardice? These are major questions in Switzerland. They touch the nature of the people and the constitutional policy of their system . . . nature and policy bearing great resemblance to my own. So my relationship to Switzerland is deep and personal, my attraction to it perhaps extreme. Here is the one system in the western world whose structure is dedicated to the freedom of MOB. It is a system which has produced great wealth and stability. You may say it is easy to be so stable when you are so wealthy. And I answer that Switzerland is not stable because she is wealthy, she is wealthy because she is stable. And you say . . . but Switzerland is so *boring*.

We should also re-examine our concept of boring. In this age of zap and multiplicity we are bored far too easily. Composer John Cage has said: 'Once there was the Mona Lisa, now we also have the Mona Lisa with a moustache.' We have become bored with a Mona Lisa without a moustache. If happiness is the absence of unhappiness (my definition), then stability is the absence of strife. Life without strife is 'boring'. Happiness is 'boring'. Paradise must be boring. What is more boring than having nothing left to strive for? Switzerland is boring because if not paradise it is a society with a minimum of strife. France, England, Spain and the United States are not boring. There are always rapes, robberies, murders, corruption, strikes and general social unrest in these countries. These are interesting events. Right now,[1] for example, there is a French postal strike paralysing the country. It has been going on for six weeks. Stories have it that the strikers are destroying mail sacks stacked in Orly Airport. The railways and domestic fuel delivery drivers are also on strike, there are power cuts, radio and television journalists are on strike, coalminers in the Lorraine, farmers are dumping rotten meat and vegetables on the roads in protest. Garbage has not been collected in Paris for three weeks. It is very interesting to live amidst out-front class warfare and as an avowed anarchist I should be sublimely happy. But there is also the smell of bitterness, impatience, aggression, a smell of occupation that is not so pleasant. The smell of the boiling-mad 49% minority. Our demands for interest have escalated along with population, inflation, and everything else. In our times, an interesting society has come to mean simply one that does not work.

I lived in Basel for two months last year helping some friends who were filming Hermann Hesse's novel, *Steppenwolf*. One day we were on location in the Gorge de Schelton in the nearby Jura. A modest, narrow, paved pass with a stream rushing down beside it. The camera and crew were being lifted by crane to a broad commanding rock. A wide spot in the pass was occupied by actors, extras, wardrobe personnel, electricians, soundmen and grips preparing the shot. I wandered down a bit. A small iron grate in the ground caught my eye. I looked more closely: it was a storm drain. These mountain roads probably flood easily. But still ... in Occitania there are few storm drains even in towns which also flood easily, and here, absolutely in the middle of nothing but trees and rocks with no sign of a house, with the nearest village five kilometres away ... a storm drain. It was numbered and not rusty. I flashed on this little old boring Swiss engineer with combed grey hair under a spotless blue cap and a pipe in his mouth pedaling a bicycle around the countryside in all seasons checking storm drains and researching the need for more. Over every kilometre of no matter how remote mountain roads, lining them all with numbered, maintained storm drains to forestall even the remotest possibility of a mess. Switzerland works.

Why does it work? Because it is small. All living in the same house as it were, it being a crowded house, there is no opportunity to shove the dirt under the rug. They keep their house in order. But this can also be said of the Danes and the Dutch. What is unique about Switzerland? When I say small I mean *small*. A country half the size of Scotland to begin with, divided into twenty-two autonomous units (cantons) each with the greatest practical freedom of MOB.

Each canton has a majority and minority of its own. Take one, for example, whose majority has voted with the losing cause in a given federal election. In France or in England, where the power lies at the centre, the majority of this local entity – a department or a county – would thus remain a minority in national terms. Here, however, since the real power lies at the local level, majority rules. There are no cultural, economic or political carpetbaggers. Minorities become majorities by simple division. Democracy is increased in direct proportion to the decrease in the size of the unit.

The Jura is a French-speaking Catholic area within the German-speaking Protestant canton of Bern with a population of 80,000, including all seven districts of which the southern three have a sizeable Germanized minority. It is a small – about 30 by 40 kilometres – arrowhead pushing into France, obviously French not German and there has been autonomist sentiment since 1815 when it was first attached to Bern. The refusal of the Public Works portfolio to a Jurassien because he spoke French led to the formation of the Jurassien Liberation Front in 1947. Liberationists have since occupied the Swiss embassy in Paris, tarred tramway tracks in Bern, dynamited Swiss Army installations and burned down homes of pro-Bernese farmers. The situation resembled that in Northern Ireland, and there were some who feared it might get similarly out of hand. Lucas Burkhardt, Finance Minister of the neighbouring canton of Basel, told me he considers it a 'colonial situation'. Cultural oppression combined with economic neglect, perfect ingredients for alienation and violence. But this is Switzerland, and finally good sense ruled and they decided to vote on it. The Swiss are for ever voting. In this case, a local case, as in all local cases, only the locals voted. Not the entire country, not even the entire canton of Bern, both would have been interference. Just the seven Jura districts. There was a total clear majority in favour of autonomy. The three southern, Germanized districts, however, voted with a slight majority against it. Instead of leaving them a discontented minority in the future canton of the Jura, they will now vote again. Not the entire Jura, just the southern three. Another minority becomes a majority. Another minority problem solved by simple division. I had to laugh just yesterday when I read in *Le Monde* that there is a new proposal suggesting the problem of a German-Protestant minority in a French-Catholic Jura be solved by forming *two* Juras, half cantons south and north. A half-canton has exactly the same rights as a full canton except that it sends only one senator to the federal Council of States instead of two. (Three

147

of the twenty-two cantons are already broken in half.) That's right, I thought . . . of course, always the same answer: break it down, the smaller the better.

When you live in Europe for a while you learn that nobody likes anybody. The French dislike the Germans, the English dislike the French. The Norwegians don't like the Swedes. Nobody likes the Belgians. Inside States, people from the north of France laugh at 'the accent' of the south; Catalonians and Basques do not like Andalusians; even inside tiny Belgium, the Flemings do not particularly care for the Walloons. Switzerland is composed of three major European groupings whose cultural homelands have been at war off and on for centuries. They do not particularly like each other. You find hostility down to the cantonal level, even to districts within a canton. They are no angels. Yet the Swiss alone have remained at peace with themselves and everybody else. They choose to remain Swiss. They know they are on to a good thing. Though Germans are a 75% majority (20% French, 4% Italian, 1% Romanche) the Swiss elected (*sic*!) a 'French' general, Henri Guisson, to be commander in chief of their defensive armed forces during World War II. If such a diverse citizenship can get along so well while infected by such hostile history, so can absolutely anybody else. Give people the freedom of MOB and the rest will fall into place. There is only one thing absolutely unique about the Swiss, other than their diversity. The freedom of MOB.

We are living in an era of flat-out Balkanization. The U.N. has more than doubled its size in a generation and is still multiplying. For those who say, all right, it's time to stop, there's a limit after all, I say on the contrary, Balkanization has not yet gone far enough. The limit is the lowest possible common denominator. The half-canton. Let's half-cantonize the world.

Let there be light. So what? How practical is all of this? How practical is Nationism? How real a force? How much of it is mere folklore? Scotland will certainly be devoluted, possibly by the time you read this. Wales will soon have some degree of autonomy. France is harder. The Occitan movement is not much of a force. Brittany, its culture buried under centuries of strict centralism, not much more. Yet the resentment against the capital is real enough and we only have to imagine major economic trouble or the discovery of oil off Brest to see the possibility of a changed equation. The Basques and the Catalans are *nations*. They are real. They are occupied. The resistance is real and will grow once fascism is lifted from Spain. The Lapps are weak and not numerous, yet they have more recognition as a nation than they had ten years ago and some degree of local government is probable. No, Nationism is real enough. The questions are only when devolution will come and how far it will go.

My one argument with Nationism is that it does not go far enough. I would rather see 12 autonomous counties than an autonomous Wales, 5 autonomous departments than an autonomous Brittany, 4 autonomous provinces than an autonomous Basque Country. Let each county, department and province decide for itself which language to speak, how to spend its own taxes, what political and economic structure it will have. The Swiss model turns out to be even better than Nationists imagine, by facing them immediately with a devolution of their own.

The Swiss are first citizens of their canton, only then are they Swiss. Direct taxes are paid to the cantons which keep 80% and pass along the rest to the federal government to pay for defence, customs, post, the diplomatic service, and so on. The rich cantons subsidize the poor. The canton of Uri, for example, has only one industry, its economy is otherwise subsistence mountain farming. With a very low population density, Uri must nevertheless bear a large financial burden maintaining the Gotthard roads. The budget of Uri is met 85% by federal subventions originating in Basel, Zurich, Geneva and Bern. This most bourgeois of countries thus spreads its wealth around like socialists. Not, note, on a class basis. Rather from MOB to MOB, leaving each MOB free to deal with its own classes in a manner of its own choosing.

The Timothy Leary episode is a good example of the cantonal system. The federal government granted Leary asylum, that is they said they would not kick him out. But the federal government does not have the power to grant residence, that is a cantonal matter. As it turned out the former high priest of L.S.D. was not respectable enough for the Swiss, no canton would accept him and he had to keep moving between temporary addresses, never staying more than a few weeks in each until he got fed up and left on his ill-fated flight to Afghanistan. Whatever one may think of the actual refusal, the principle seems sound. People have the right to decide which aliens they want living next door.

This opens a Pandora's box. What about bussing, and integration in the American South? It is difficult . . . shaky ground . . . but keep in mind that most southern states in America are at least twice the size of Switzerland itself and the situation is consequently not strictly comparable. When I say local I mean *local*. Half-cantonal. Local enough to make a minority truly and justly minor, local enough to have a shared ethical vision. We also must be prepared to pay a price for the freedom of MOB. MOBs will sometimes not be terribly enlightened. One federal function should be their enlightenment. But people ought to have the right to deal with their own racists and local racists are less dangerous than those with their hands on centralized power.

When a city official of Basel has a problem to discuss with his counterpart in Mulhouse or some other French border town, the French official must first check with Paris before arranging a meeting. Or else they meet clandestinely, at some out-of-the-way restaurant. Another comparison between a devoluted society and centralism. Using any measure you want, which is more efficient? Left and right has absolutely nothing to do with it.

The Canton of Graubunden (Grisons) – everything has two or three names in Switzerland, even the country itself– Schweiz, Suisse, Svizzera – is a large, under-populated, remote and relatively poor canton bordering on Austria, Italy and Liechtenstein. Many of its valleys are still cut off (by road) from each other in winter. Most of them speak German, others speak Italian and French, and 30,000 still speak Romanche. The tourist trade around some of the chickest ski stations in the world – St Moritz, Davos, Klosters – has brought in the outside world with a vengeance. English is more common than Romanche during the season. Romanche descends directly from 'Vulgar' Latin, it predates early

French. It was made the fourth official language (by popular vote) in reaction to events just prior to World War II. Hitler had incorporated German Switzerland into the Third Reich on official maps. Anyone who spoke German was German as far as Hitler was concerned. Mussolini felt the same way about Italian. The French have always felt that way about French. The Swiss figured they had better hold on to something of their own. The federal government has been pumping in subsidies ever since, though young people in Graubunden prefer to speak German and Romanche seems to be going the way of Breton and Welsh.

A central government preserving its most minor culture, not killing it, paying and going to a lot of trouble to preserve an archaic, dying, 'inefficient' folklorique situation. Swiss diversity is its unity, it is even considered somewhat un-Swiss to be too Swiss. Anyone holding that too many languages cause confusion and inefficiency, that diversity causes disunity should consider the Swiss.

Let me make it clear that it is not the Swiss people I am pushing, but their *system*. Man is fallen, man knows evil, the Swiss people not the least of them. Money is never far at the back of Swiss minds. Though they are proud of their tradition of granting political asylum, one finds few poor refugees in the streets of Geneva. Solvent refugees preferred, those who are prepared to work – the Swiss *WORK* – better yet those who can lend a little class to the place at the same time. Lenin had Swiss asylum, the anarchist ·Bakunin died in Swiss asylum, Solzhenitsyn has Swiss asylum now. The Swiss like to attract artistic refugees to compensate for the poor production of their own.

Swiss artists find Switzerland a good place to be *from*. Paul Klee worked in Germany. Arthur Honegger worked, and died, in Paris. Le Corbusier worked out of a French home office. On the other hand German Hermann Hesse wrote some of his best novels in Swiss asylum. And consider that if the Swiss have not produced many great artists, perhaps this is due to the nature of the people rather than their system.

It must be said that the Swiss have a collective guilt complex. This has to do with the implied coupling of neutrality and cowardice, isolationism and selfishness. They also have a collective inferiority complex, their culture being considered inferior to that of neighbouring cousins who speak the same languages. All of this results in a collective psychosis, the fear of foreigners. Despite a reputation (and flourishing business) as friendly hotel-keepers, they consider that all evil comes from foreigners. Anything and anybody from outside their tidy little country is somehow unclean, untrustworthy and probably threatening. The Swiss belong neither to the Common Market nor the United Nations. These complexes have produced the Action Party, sponsors of a recent initiative to throw out half of the current total of one million foreign workers (30% of the active population, 17% of all Swiss), mostly Italian. Any citizen collecting 50,000 signatures can propose such an initiative to popular vote. In this case it was sponsored by the most narrow, xenophobic and perhaps racist elements of the population, but 50,000 people are a large minority and they have the right to be heard. They put up their proposition and it was sensibly defeated. If the Basques had the freedom to vote on how many Andalusians should be allowed to work in the Basque Country there would be no Basque problem.

One nice thing about using the Swiss system as a model for revolution is its very bourgeois nature. Nobody can call me an irresponsible radical. I throw the centralists' values back in their face. Just look at this country which is so successful on your own terms, and wonder what makes it so successful. And on my terms, more or less anarchistic, it comes as close as any system I know to 'a voluntary agreement among individuals and groups'. Half the Swiss don't even know who their president is. Ask one and he will likely scratch his head with a wry smile: 'Ah . . . Ernst Brugger I think.' It doesn't really matter, because he is more a chairman than a president and in any case will have been rotated out of office by the time you read this. Yet at the same time there are rigid laws, Germanic order. Every Swiss is a cop; make an illegal U-turn and motorists flash their lights at you in disapproval. Private property is sacred, they do not share easily. You are expected to work your way. Owe too much money or get caught playing around with it in a way likely to hurt national profits and you go immediately to jail. No passing go. Remember Edith Irving and Bernie Cornfeld. When I asked a Swiss film producer friend of mine about these contradictions, unable to resolve them, he finally just shook his head and said: 'There is no Switzerland. Switzerland doesn't exist.'

The name of the Marxist magazine in Geneva is *Tout Va Bien* ('Everything is fine'). Interviewing some of the young radicals from the magazine, I asked what there was for a Swiss Marxist to militate for. They laughed at my innocence and said there were plenty of inequities in Swiss society. The old, for example, are left uncared for with a pension of only 600 Swiss francs a month which is not enough to live on. Foreign workers are poorly treated, they do not have the right to strike and their housing is deplorable. There are too many nuclear power plants, not enough awareness of the ecological implications. But these are worldwide problems, not any worse here than anywhere else and I could not prod them into remembering any others. There was not much talk about class warfare. (Unemployment had just doubled, from 40 to 80). They complained in general about the mercenary nature of Swiss society, but while perhaps more acute it is also more up-front. No beating about the bush, there is a political party in Geneva called bluntly the 'Bourgeois Party'. And avarice is not peculiarly Swiss.

One of the young directors of *Tout Va Bien* teaches at the university and recently almost lost his job because of his outspoken Marxism. He called the Minister of Education in Bern to discuss the problem. The Marxist is French-Swiss, the Minister German. The Minister gave him an appointment for the following morning. Not a secretary or an assistant, the Minister himself, and not next month but tomorrow morning. The young Marxist admitted that this was not unique, Swiss officials are generally available. I said that it was rather a healthy situation.

'Yeah, I guess so,' he said sheepishly.

'It must be pretty hard to stay militant here,' I said.

He shrugged his shoulders even more sheepishly: 'Oh, what do you want me to say? It works. The bloody thing works.'

Appendix A
Jean-Paul Sartre's
'The Burgos Trials'[1]

If the newspapers are to be believed the Burgos trials have
caused a sensation by bringing to light the grotesque ferocity
of the Franco regime. But, really did we need any fresh proof
of fascist savagery? Since 1936 imprisonment, torture and
execution have been commonplace throughout the Iberian
Peninsula. What the trials have done is to arouse consciences
inside and outside of Spain by revealing to many people for
the first time the existence of the Basque nation, and
established this fact as by no means unique. All big nations
contain interior colonies within frontiers they themselves have
drawn.

Shackled and muzzled though they were, the men of
Burgos, instead of having to fight for their lives, succeeded in
turning the trial into a test of decentralisation. To take
another European example, French children are taught that
the history of France consists in the unification of all 'our'
provinces, begun by the Kings, carried on by the French
Revolution and completed in the nineteenth century. When I
was at school I was taught to be proud of this. The attainment
of national unity, once it had been achieved, explained the
perfection of our language and the universality of our culture.
Whatever our political views, this was beyond challenge. On
this point, socialists and communists were at one with
conservatives. Whether reformers or revolutionaries, they all
considered themselves heirs of jacobin centralism, they took
the Hexagon as a unity to which they wished to bring the
benefits of a new regime. Certain things were so and could not
be changed. The absolute monarchy had evolved along with
the development of roads and means of communication, with

the invention of artillery, and with the mercantilist needs of the capital. The revolution and jacobinism had enabled the bourgeoisie now in power to further the unification of the economy by levelling feudal and ethnic barriers and to win foreign wars with mass armies levied without regard to ethnic origins. The nineteenth century had completed this work by industrialisation and its consequences of rural depopulation, concentration and the new ideology, bourgeois nationalism. The present unity was in fact the historic achievement of the dominant class and had produced everywhere between the Belgian and Spanish Frontiers the same type of abstract man defined by the same formal rights – democracy – and the same real obligations, without taking any account of his concrete necessities. Nobody questioned this. Hence the stupefaction of December 1970.

The trial was infamous and ridiculous, but could one reject the validity of the charges brought against the accused without at the same time acknowledging the validity of ETA's objections? Of course, the Spanish government is fascist and this complicated matters. Most people could protest against the Franco regime with a clear conscience. But they then had to support the accused and ETA who said, 'We are not only against Franco, we are first and foremost against "Spain".' This was a bitter pill to swallow. They could not acknowledge that a Basque nation existed on the other side of the Pyrenees without conceding the right of 'our' Basques to integration with them. And after that, what about Brittany, Alsace, Occitania? As Morvan Lebesque recently said, the history of France would have to be written backwards. Du Guesclin, hero of Centralism, would have to figure simply as a traitor to the Breton cause. The Burgos trials drew attention to a new fact, the gradual re-birth everywhere of what centralist governments call 'Separatism'. In the USSR, many republics, especially the Ukraine, are troubled by centrifugal forces. Sicily recently achieved separate status. In Yugoslavia, France, Spain, Northern Ireland, Belgium, Canada and elsewhere, social conflicts have begun to take on an ethnic dimension. Provinces declare themselves nations and more or less openly claim the status of nations. It has become clear that the present frontiers correspond to the interests of the dominant classes and not to popular aspirations, that the unity of which the great powers are so proud is a cloak for the oppression of peoples and for the overt or covert use of repressive violence.

There are two obvious reasons for the revitalisation of nationalist movements. First the atomic revolution. Morvan Lebesque tells of a leading Breton nationalist who on hearing of Hiroshima cried out 'At last the Breton problem exists'. Up till that moment, centralism was reinforced and justified by the threat of one country against another. In the age of the atomic bomb this blackmail has no force. The centralism of the cold war, the power of Washington and Moscow, holds sway over nations, not provinces. Suddenly, while some nations hasten to join one or the other bloc, other smaller nations regain consciousness of their identity and no longer feel integrated. The second reason, related to the first, is the process of decolonisation which since the last war has spread over three continents.

Imagine a young man from the department of Finistère in Brittany doing his national service in North Africa in 1960. They tell him that it's to support a police action, to suppress an insane criminal agitation in some overseas departments. Then, behold, the French are routed and abandon these departments. They retreat from them and recognise Algeria as a sovereign nation. What now does it mean to the demobilised soldier that he belongs to Finistère? He has seen in Algeria that the departments are abstract divisions, serving to disguise conquest by force and colonisation. Why shouldn't the same apply on this side of the Mediterranean, in 'metropolitan' France? Finistère disappears as an abstraction, a mere administrative convenience. He feels himself to be Breton, no more and no less, and French only by conquest. Is he going to resign himself to being colonised? If not, the examples of Algeria and Vietnam are there to impel him to revolt. The victories in Vietnam, above all, teach him that the colonisers have cleverly narrowed the field of possibilities for him and his brothers. They have made him a deviant. They have taught him that as a Frenchman he has the same right to vote as the inhabitant of any other province, as a Breton he cannot raise a finger, much less fight against the central power, which can annihilate him effortlessly. But in Indo-China, poor peasants threw the French into the sea and have fought successfully against the greatest military power in the capitalist world. This too, was impossible. The field of possibilities is suddenly enlarged for him. What if the colonisers are only paper tigers?

Atomic fission and decolonisation have rekindled a new patriotism among conquered peoples. Everybody basically realises this, but there are those in France and Spain and Canada who think that this will to independence is a mere caprice, nourished on false analogies, and that the separatist movements will disappear of their own accord. But now the example of the Basques is here to show us that this rebirth is not a casual thing but a necessity. It could not have taken place if the so-called provinces had not had a national existence which for centuries the conquerors had tried to suppress and obstruct and conceal, but had remained in being, an historic and fundamental tie between the people.

If this link, tacitly acknowledged by the central government, does not justify an inferior status for a conquered land, then that people will wage a fierce struggle for self-determination.

If we read our history without centralist prejudices, clearly the Basque people differ from all surrounding peoples and have never lost the consciousness of their singularity, defined by physical characteristics and preserved by the difference between their language, Euskerra, and all Indo-European languages. In the seventh century the Duchy of Vasconia was the home of a mountain people who defeated the army of Charlemagne at Roncevalles. By the year 1000 it had become the Kingdom of Navarre, but from the 12th century was in decline. In 1515, Spain took possession. Despite or perhaps because of that conquest, the Basque consciousness increased. It was still largely a feudal age, Spanish centralism was weak and the vanquished retained from the middle ages certain rights, the *Fueros*, long to be a bastion of resistance. But people become discontented with this restricted autonomy, and did not lose hope of regaining their independence. When Napoleon was re-fashioning Europe, a deputation from Biscay proposed to him the establishment of an independent Basque state inside the Empire, but in vain. The constitution of 1812 almost abolished the *Fueros* and the nationalist movement wasted itself in a blind attempt to bring back the past. Isabel II was more liberal but still a centraliser in the French Style, so that popular forces sided with Don Carlos, the absolutist Pretender, who was more old-fashioned but whose love of the past made him wish to restore the feudal autonomy of Navarre. Both Carlist wars were lost. In 1879 the *Fueros* were abolished, and there arose a zealot traditionalism, the legacy of the sword.

Six years later Sabino Aranda formed the PNV – the Basque National Party – bourgeois and intellectual. There was now no question of fighting for absolutism and the restoration of the *Fueros*. The PNV was politically progressive, aiming at independence, but socially conservative, even antiquated – one of its slogans was 'God and the old laws'. Basque resistance so shocked the Spaniards that some of them including the anarchist Pi-y-Margall, proposed a federalist solution for the problems of the Peninsula. Later, during the Republic, the plan was adopted and the central government recognised the principle of regional autonomy on condition that 70 per cent of the inhabitants concerned voted for it in a referendum. Upper Navarre was essentially rural and attached to Carlism. The Carlists promptly took up arms for Franco and the Navarrese voted against autonomy, though what they were really voting against was not autonomy but the Republic. The other three Basque provinces voted overwhelmingly in favour of autonomy.

The Republican government turned out to be more centralist than it had at first seemed, and needlessly held things up until 1936. Autonomy was now conceded but under pressure of events and for essentially practical and military reasons. The Basque country had to be won over for armed resistance to Franco's coup. So the Basque government was established, three socialist, two liberals and one communist. This showed that the influence of the PNV extended to the most diverse strata of society, and that it had modified its initial conservatism. Until April 1937 Basque troops ferociously defended the provinces of Guipuzcoa and Biscay. We know the rest. Franco sends up reinforcements, the reign of terror, the bombing of Guernica, 1,500 dead. August 1937 was the last month of the Republic of Euskadi.

After the war came repression, imprisonment, torture, executions. President Aguirre, leader of the PNV, fled to France. During the Second World War he played the cards of the democracies, hoping that Franco would follow Hitler and Mussolini into defeat. Today we can see his innocence and our shame. The PNV was played out and has been in constant decline since 1945. However in 1947, hoping to involve its allies, it fomented a general strike. The allies did not move, they stood by while Franco put it down with an implacable repression. It was the end of the road for the PNV, which retains a certain prestige as the 'historic' party which gave birth to the short-lived Basque Republic, but today has no potential for action. Its methods do not correspond to the situation, the exiles are growing old and Aguirre is dead. But none of this matters. ETA has arisen to take the place of the old bourgeois party. Let this brief resumé show that the Basques, a people only *recently* conquered by Spain, have always fiercely rejected integration. If the Basques could vote today I believe that by an overwhelming majority they would choose independence.

Can we say with ETA, that Euskadi is a colony of Spain? The question is important, for it is in colonies that the class struggle and the national struggle merge. Under the colonial system, the colonised countries supply raw materials and food products for the industrial metropolis, and the workers are underpaid. But the Basque country, especially the provinces of Guipuzcoa and Biscay have, since the beginning of this century been fully developed industrially. In 1960 the consumption of electrical energy per inhabitant per annum was 2,008 Kw. in these two provinces. In Spain and Catalonia it was 658 Kw. The figure for Spain alone would be lower still, but official statistics deliberately take Catalonia jointly with Spain in order to create intentional confusion. Steel production per head of the population is 860 kilos, in Biscay, 450 for all Euskadi, 45 in Spain-and-Catalonia. In Guipuzcoa 9.45 per cent of the population work in the primary sector, 56.8 per cent in the secondary sector, 33.75 per cent in the tertiary sector. For Biscay the proportions are 8.6, 57.5, 33.9 per cent. By contrast, in Spain-and-Catalonia the primary sector employs 43.5 per cent of the workers, the secondary sector 27.2 per cent and the tertiary 29.3 per cent. The considerable growth of the last two sectors, plus the fact that in these provinces the rural population is consistently decreasing, shows the enormous potential of the Basque country for industrial development. From this point of view Biscay and Gupuzcoa are the pilot regions of the Iberian Peninsula. And here we come up against the paradox that, if this is a colonial situation, the colonising country is poor and mainly agricultural while the colonised country is rich and displays the demographic profile of a highly industrialised society.

But at second glance the paradox is more apparent than real. Euskadi may be prosperous but its population is only two million, it had fewer in 1514 and in those days the population was rural. The conquest happened because of the much greater population of the other country. On the other bank of the Bidassoa the French Basque country, similar in structure to Upper Navarre (in Spain) has been systematically pillaged, ruined and depopulated by the French conquerors. Here colonialism is much more apparent. Obviously the lethargy of 'Spain' during the first thirty years of this century allowed Euskadi to ensure for itself a flourishing economy with Bilbao as the focal point. But the question is, who profits by this economy? One answer is that history offers no example of a conquered country which does not pay tribute to the conqueror. But official sources supply a better answer. These prove that 'Spain' is committed to a veritable campaign of fiscal pillage against the Basque country. The workers are crushed by taxes. In Guipuzcoa these are the highest in the peninsula.

And that is not all. In all the 'Spanish' provinces the government puts in more than it takes out in taxes, 150 per cent in Toledo, 151 per cent in Burgos, 164 per cent in Avila, etc. The two industrialised provinces of the Basque country pay to the foreign government that exploits them 4,338,400,000 pesetas. The Spanish state puts into Euskadi 774,000,000 pesetas, stealing 3,000,500,000 pesetas for the benefit of the Castilian desert. Moreover, most of the 774,000,000 pesetas go to maintain the apparatus of oppression (a Spanish or hispanicised administration, army of occupation, police, courts, etc.) or of deBasquisation (the University where only Spanish language and culture are taught). The main problem of Basque industry is that of productivity. To achieve competitive prices in the world markets it must import modern machinery, but the Spanish state is largely autoarchic and forbids this. The Madrid money market discriminates against Biscay and favours Castille. The ports of Bilbao and Pasajes need to be adapted and equipped for big ships. A considerable construction programme is essential for them, as for the fishing ports, but nothing has been done. Likewise the 'Spanish' railway system is a serious drawback. The direct road distance between Bilbao, and Vitoria is 66 Km, the journey by rail is 137 Km. But the administration and the INI (The National Institute of Industry), the organ of the oppressor state, is manned by ignorant and stubborn bureaucrats who understand none of the country's needs, largely because they consider it to be, at least in theory, a Spanish province, and obstruct the necessary improvements, while 'Spain' makes no attempt to absorb the uncompetitive products.

Tariffs are inversely preferential, preventing the lowering of certain costs and procuring the privilege of consuming Basque products without correspondingly increased profit to the producer. The consequence is inevitable. Per capita revenue is among the highest in the Peninsula (though that is not saying much), but the income of wage earners (85 per cent of the active population) is lower than that of those in Madrid, Burgos, Valencia, etc. It must be pointed out that the rates of wage increases between 1955 and 1967, were for Spain 6.3 per cent, for Euskadi 4.1 per cent. So despite the over-industrialisation of the country, there are two essential factors in a classical example of colonialism: pillage, fiscal or other, of the colonised country and super-exploitation of the workers.

To these may be added a third, which proceeds from the first two, the rhythm of emigration and immigration. The Spanish government has taken advantage of the necessities of industrialisation to direct to Euskadi unskilled labour from the more backward regions. It has offered them such inducements as housing priority. Super-exploited like the

Basques, but without an evolved class consciousness, they are peons at the disposal of the bosses. Out of a population of between 1,800,000 and 2,000,000, between 300,000 and 351,000 are estimated to be immigrants. On the other hand there is Basque emigration from the poorer regions, especially Navarre. Between 150,000 and 200,000 Basques live in Madrid of whom about 100,000 are from Navarre. This considerable blood-letting, together with the influx of Spanish workers into the industrial regions may be considered as a principle of colonial destruction.

This consistent fascist policy clearly involves the complicity of the large employers of Biscay and Guipuzcoa. Ever since an upper bourgeoisie began to appear in Bilbao after the Carlist Wars, they have always been liberal and centralist. The registered offices of their big companies have moved to Madrid. They can only see advantages in the curbing of modernisation by Spanish incompetence and autarchy. The vast Spanish market can absorb their uncompetitive products on a global scale. The management is assured of a high percentage of profit without being obliged to invest heavily. Strangers to the true interests of the nation, these collaborationists, whose centralism spells ruin to the Basque economy, have excluded themselves from the community of the nation, and play the role of what has been called the *comprador*. In the final analysis, and within the framework of the centralist system they find their advantages in a certain malthusianism.

The conclusion is clear. Despite appearances, the situation of the Basque wage earner is in all aspects that of a colonialised worker. He is not merely exploited, as the Castilian worker is exploited, who wages a 'chemically pure' class struggle, but deliberately super-exploited, in that he does the same work as the Spanish worker and receives a lower wage for it. There is super-exploitation of the country by the central government with the complicity of the compradors who, on the basis of this super-exploitation, themselves exploit the workers. Super-exploitation does not benefit the Basque capitalists, simple exploiters overburdened by taxes and protected by a foreign army which only benefits 'Spain', that is to say a fascist society propped up by American imperialism. The working classes however are not always conscious of this super-exploitation, and many wage earners dreamed until recently of identifying with the claims of workers of Madrid and Burgos. This would only have led them into a negative centralism. They have to be made to understand that in the case of Euskadi, the economic and social problems are expressed in national terms. When the country no longer pays fiscal tribute to the occupying power, when its true problems are formulated and dealt with in Bilbao and Pamplona, not in Madrid, then the economic structure can be freely transformed.

We repeat, 'Spain' super-exploits the Basques *because they are Basques.* Without ever officially admitting it, they are convinced that the Basques are *distinct,* ethnically and culturally. Do they believe that all memory of the Carlist Wars, the Republic of 1936 and the strikes of 1947 has been expunged? If no such memories were left, would there be such interest in destroying the Basque language? Here clearly is a colonialist technique. For a hundred years the French tried to destroy Arabic in Algeria. They did not succeed, but at least they made literary Arabic into a dead language which is no longer taught. They have done the same thing, relatively successfully, with Basque in Lower Navarre and Breton in Brittany.

Thus on both sides of the frontier there has been an attempt to make an identical people believe that their language is merely a dialect and a dying one at that. In Southern ('Spanish') Euskadi its use is virtually prohibited. No Basque medium schools are allowed, publication in the language is being eliminated, schools and the University teach the language and culture of the oppressor. Radio, films, television and the press explain in Spanish the problems of 'Spain', they are all propaganda organs of the Madrid government. The administrative personnel are all Spanish or hispanicised, chosen by examinations organised in Spanish by Madrid bureaucrats. For this reason, for the reason that the foreigner has willed it, one hears it said in Bilbao, 'The Basque language and culture are of no use.' And the press often repeats an unfortunate remark of Unamuno, 'The Basque language will soon die out'.

163

But even this is not all. In the schools, children are punished for talking in Basque. Peasants may speak it in the villages, but would never think of doing so in big towns. One of the accused at Burgos was allowed to receive visits from his father while in prison, but permission was withdrawn when he spoke Basque, not out of provocation but because he knew no other language. The forcible suppression of the Basque language is cultural genocide. It is one of the oldest languages in Europe. True, it emerged at a time when the economy of the entire continent was rural, and if it has not adapted itself to the evolution of society, this is because the Spanish conqueror has prohibited its use. In order that it may become a twentieth century language – and to some extent it already has – it must be spoken.

Hebrew and Breton have had the same difficulties and have solved them. An Israeli can talk about nuclear fision and read the Dead Sea Scrolls as we read Racine and Corneille. Morvan Lebesque claims that Breton has a modern vocabulary formed more regularly than that of French, the 'national' language. An ancient language which has remained young because its development has been arrested will have considerable resources. If Basque were to become the national language of Euskadi it would carry within itself all the riches of its past, a special way of thinking and feeling, and would enrich the present and the future. What the Spaniard wants is for it to disappear, and with it the Basque personality. The inhabitant of Biscay who talks Euskerra makes himself into a Basque, not only because he regains a past that belongs to him, and him alone, but because it leads him, although he may be alone, into the community of all those who speak the language.

In Burgos, the final speeches of the accused were delivered in Euskerra. They rejected the claim of the tribunal to sit in judgment on them when it did not even understand them. In doing so they summoned the entire nation into the hall of judgment. And, although unseen, in that moment it stood there with them.

The official account of the trial records at this point that the accused made unintelligible statements in a language which 'appeared to be Basque'. Marvellous! The judges understood nothing, but they knew what it was about. They could not bring themselves to admit that the Basque nation had invaded the courtroom, so they reduced Euskerra to the status of a 'probable' language, so obscure that no one knew whether the speaker was really using it or was making meaningless sounds. The language is the arrow of Basque culture and the grand preoccupation of the oppressors. If they succeed in destroying the language, the Basque will become the abstract man they want him to be. He will speak Spanish, which is not and never has been his language. But as this does not mean that he will cease to be super-exploited, once he becomes conscious of colonialism, Euskerra revives.

The converse is also true. *For him to speak his own language is a revolutionary act.* The conscious Basque of today goes still further, when he talks about the culture it gives him and that he wishes it to give him. Culture, he will say, is a creation by man for man. But he will add that there cannot be a universal culture while universal oppression remains unbroken. The official culture in Euskadi today is universalist, in that it seeks to make the Basque into a universal man, deprived of all his natural idiosyncracies, an abstract citizen similar in every respect to the Spaniard, except that he is super-exploited and does not realise it. In this sense, the only universalism he shares is that of oppression. But however exploited men are, they do not become *things*. On the contrary, they fashion themselves into the negation of the contradictions that are imposed on them. Thus the Basque must be the negation of the Spaniard that they have tried to turn him into. Not an abstract negation, but a microcosm of all they know that is special to themselves and their environment. In this sense, Basque culture today must be a counter-culture, aimed at the destruction of Spanish culture and the rejection of the universalist humanism of the centralist powers. It is a strong and continuing effort to win back to Basque reality – the landscape, ecology, ethnic characteristics, literature in Euskerra, which is clearly visible but disguised by the oppressor as harmless folklore for foreign tourists. So they add a third formula, Basque culture is the *praxis* which will get rid of the oppression of man by man in the Basque country. And conversely this work must lead out into a political praxis, since Basque man cannot fully express himself until his country is sovereign.

Thus, by inexorable dialectic, conquest, centralisation and super-exploitation have resulted in the maintenance and strengthening of the Basque claim to independence by the very forces that Spain has used to suppress it. We can now try to determine the precise necessities of the concrete situation, that is, the nature of the Basque people's fight today. There are two different responses to Spanish oppression, both of them inadequate. We may identify them as the Basque Communist Party (PC) and the PNV.

PC regards Euskadi as merely a geographical expression. It takes its orders from the Spanish Communist Party in Madrid and takes no account of local realities. Clinging to centralism, it is socially progressive and politically conservative. It attempts to lead the Basque workers into the 'chemically pure' class struggle. They forget they are dealing with a colonised, super-exploited country.

Despite certain opportunist declarations of support for ETA during the Burgos trials, PC does not understand that the actions it proposes have inadequate objectives and hence cannot succeed. If the Basques merely struggle against exploitation as such, they abandon their own problems in order to help the Spanish workers to eliminate the Franco bourgeoisie. They would thus cease to be Basques. They would be working towards a socialist society for abstract, universalist man who is the product of centralising capitalism. And when that man is in power in Madrid and controls the means of production will the Basques be able to count on him, to grant them autonomy? Highly unlikely: he saw what it cost the Republic, and socialist countries today are willing colonisers. Against super-exploitation and consequent deBasquisation, the Basques have to *fight alone*. This does not rule out *tactical* alliances with other revolutionary movements working to undermine the Franco dictatorship. But there can be no common strategy. The fight will be a solitary one. It will be against 'Spain', not the Spanish people, for a colonised nation can only put an end to super-exploitation by making itself sovereign vis-a-vis the coloniser.

The PNV is also mistaken. It considers independence as an end in itself. First, they say, let us set up the Basque Republic, then we can change our society any way we like. But if this means setting up a bourgeois Basque state then, although Spanish super-exploitation would be brought to an end, it would not be long before the new state fell into the clutches of American Imperialism. If the state retained the structure of capitalism the *compradors* would sell the country, the USA would rule through the local bourgeoisie, colonialism would be succeeded by neo-colonialism. Super-exploitation, although disguised, would not be lessened. Only a socialist society, because of its rigorous control of the economy, can establish economic relations with other nations, capitalist or communist, and then only at great risk, as the history of relations between Cuba and the USSR clearly shows.

The inadequacy of both PC and PNV responses demonstrates, in the case of Euskadi, that independence and socialism are two sides of the same coin. Thus the fight for socialism and the fight for independence must be the same fight. And if this is so, obviously the working class, who, as we have seen, are in the majority, must assume the leadership of the struggle. The worker, by becoming conscious of super-exploitation, and thus of his nationality, fulfils his vocation as a socialist. Can this be said to have happened? That is something we will deal with later. On the other hand the situation of the colonised country is such that many people in the middle classes reject cultural depersonalisation without always realising the social consequences which this rejection implies. They are, in principle, the allies of the proletariat. A revolutionary movement in a colony if it is conscious of its task, will not be inspired by the concept of 'class against class' which only makes sense in a metropolitan country, but will accept the lower middle class and the intellectuals, on condition that the revolutionaries sprung from the middle classes align themselves under the leadership of the working class. Thus the work to be done consists in a dual and progressive enlightenment. The proletariat must first become aware of its colonised condition.

The other classes, more committedly nationalist, must understand that for a colonised nation, socialism is the only possible avenue to sovereignty. For these reasons, the independence party has evolved over 150 years, changing its orientation. Instead of its nostalgic striving to re-establish the ancient *fueros* in the bosom of an absolutist state, it must aim at building a sovereign and socialist society. And it must adjust to another peculiarity of the Iberian Peninsula, which gives a special character to the Basque struggle. Centralist unification, as in Italy and Germany, was not completed until the nineteenth century and thus took the form of a Fascist dictatorship which reacts, and can only react, to separatist claims by violence and in no other way.

In two of these three countries, fascism is no longer in power, but Franco is still the Candillo of Spain. That is what a Basque meant when he said to me 'we have the horrible fate of Francoism'. Horrible it certainly is. But why fate? If Spain were a bourgeois democracy the situation would be more ambiguous. The regime would be dilatory, full of false promises and reforms. This would undoubtedly create an important sector of reformists among the Basques which would be allied to the oppressor and would be content with concessions and a federal status. Since 1937, the blind brutality of Franco has exposed the futility of reformist illusions. Every claim has always met with the same answer: bloody repression. We should not be surprised that the regime should behave in this way. But this regime is the reality of Spain the coloniser. Whatever form it takes, the government of centralist Spain, will totally reject Basque claims and will by the last analysis drown every Basque revolt in blood. Spaniards, in that they are themselves the creation of centralist idealism, are abstract men, they believe that all inhabitants of the peninsula find this logical except a handful of agitators.

Do they really believe it? Obviously not. They know that Euskadi exists, but they prefer to ignore it. They get annoyed when the Basques affirm themselves as such, and end up by hating them as Basques, that is as concrete men. The holders of power also know that the end of the colonial regime in Euskadi would bring greater misery to Castile and Andalusia. A republic would have to do the same thing as Franco. The 'fate' that the Franco regime represents for the Basques is this: it shows clearly the true nature of colonialism. It does not discuss, it oppresses or kills. Since oppressive violence is inevitable the colonials have no choice but to meet violence with violence. Temptations to reformism have no place. The Basque people must be radicalised. They know that independence can only be obtained by armed struggle. The Burgos trial was clear on this point. When they confronted the 'Spaniards' the accused knew that they risked imprisonment, torture and death. They knew it and they fought. Not in the hope of throwing out the oppressor immediately, but to contribute to the build-up of a clandestine army. If PNV is in decline it is because it has only superficially understood Fascism. The Basques have no other alternative but a people's war. Independence or death, yesterday's motto in Cuba and Algeria, is today's motto in Euskadi. Armed struggle for an independent and socialist Euskadi is what the present situation demands. Either that or submission, which is unthinkable.

From 1947 to 1959 it was an empty, unanswered demand. But in reality it was at work inside the Basque people, especially the young. In 1953 it all began. A group of intellectuals founded EKIN. Barely conscious of the true reality of the Basque problem in all its tragic simplicity, they yet understood the necessity for recourse to new and radical action. They were soon obliged to merge with the PNV which, although inert, was still important. But they became distinguished for taking up 'extremist' positions, and one of them was soon expelled as a 'communist'. The group promptly left the PNV en bloc out of solidarity, convinced by experience that the struggle waged by the old party since 1936 had petered out in mere words. In 1959 the group became the nucleus of a new party, ETA – Euskadi Ta Askatasuna.

At first, before taking up a theoretical position, ETA reflected the two tendencies that divided the country – the nationalist claims and the workers' revolt. From 1960 it came to be understood that in daily practice the two struggles must be united, the one strengthened by the other, and carried on jointly by the same organisations. Slowly and surely the position was clarified. In the 1960's there were violent crises. The 'humanist' right resigned. The 'universalist' left was expelled after trying to abandon the anti-colonialist struggle in order to wage, with the Spanish workers, the 'chemically pure' class war. These defections define the line much more clearly than could the writings of a hundred theorists. Still, after the purges, ETA strove to define its theories until 1968. On this level its principles are clear, they are the objective necessities of the situation as progressively revealed by the internal struggles with the rightist and left-centralists.

The ETA campaign is waged on four fronts: the workers, cultural, political, military. They function simultaneously and under common leadership, but remain separate. On the workers' front the struggle in 1969 was to get closer to the workers, who were often stubborn, and the organisation of a vanguard nucleus inside the working class. On the cultural front, ETA attacked the weakest link, the dehumanising universalism of the oppressor government. It has created *ikastolas*, nursery and primary schools where the education is exclusively through the medium of Basque. 15,000 children were in these schools in 1968-9. It has launched a literacy campaign among adults, created committees of students who agitate, by demonstrations, strikes and sit-ins, for the creation of a Basque university. It promotes Basque artists, writers, painters, singers and sculptors who go around the villages with exhibitions, popular songs, and street performances – direct theatre. In 1966 it began organising schools where the workers are taught marxism-leninism.

On the political front, which works closely with the military front, ETA politicises the entire Basque people, teaching it the scandal of repression. This is what explains the present direction of the armed struggle. The objective is not as yet to expel the oppressor but to mobilise the Basques towards the gradual build up of a clandestine army of liberation. Nevertheless since 1970 a new tendency has emerged in favour of the demilitarisation of ETA and more emphasis on political action by Basque workers. The Militants of this school believe that the commitment of ETA to the armed struggle, and the total secrecy that this must involve, runs the risk of isolating them from the working masses and so works against the ends they seek. The present tactic may be described as a spiral: action-repression-action, each action producing a brutal repression which shows the naked face of Fascist centralism, opening the eyes of an ever-increasing section of the people and so facilitating the undertaking of still more important actions.

We cannot give a better example of this form of struggle than the dialectical chain of events which reached a provisional culmination in the Burgos trials. From beginning to end of the proceedings, ETA called the shots and emerged triumphant, thus demonstrating the soundness of its tactics. At first however this was not obvious. After the massacres of 1936 and the repression of 1937, the Basque country lay crushed under Franco's repressive peace. Against this, the PNV, as we have seen, organised the strike of 1947, an action without real substance which provoked the terrible repression that silenced PNV.

But out of this very debacle the younger generation took over, and began to understand the necessity to go over to the armed struggle. ETA served notice of its existence in 1961 by its first military action. Crude bombs went off all over the place and an attempt was made to sabotage a train. This inexperienced effort brought down a brutal repression. 135 militants were detained. And so the infernal cycle, action – repression – action, was set in motion. But for a few years the 'forces of order' were made fools of. ETA could not be brought under control. Bombs went off throughout the land. Only in the spring of 1968 did the Chief of Police publish a communiqué in the Bilbao press declaring a state of hot war against ETA. The man-hunts began, but a few days later an explosion blocked the route of the 'Tour of Spain' cycle races. ('Let them take another road. They have no business here'). In June a Civil Guard was shot in the street. A few hours later, other Civil Guards, on highway patrol fired at random at a suspect and killed him. He was Javier Echebarrieta, one of the leaders of ETA. Repression spread to the clandestine movement and to the general public. Masses for the memory of Echebarrieta were prohibited, alienating the village clergy and the people. Since then intensified repression has provoked a response which could arouse the people fundamentally. Three months later the notorious police torturer Manzanas, active in Euskadi for thirty years, was executed on his own front doorstep . . .

As had been foreseen this action provoked a vile and savage

repression. It brought the people into open opposition to the authorities. The government could not accept the liquidation of its representatives, it had to find guilty men, stage a trial, demand death. But, as the 'victim' had been a hangman, most of the country would not disapprove of this execution which was a just punishment. The government thus fell into a contradiction it could not get out of. According to its point of view, which it could not change, there had to be intimidatory sanctions, but the publicity of the trial made it clear to everybody that it was a travesty of justice. The accused were selected at random from among the detainees or among those thought to be ETA leaders. Under these conditions the trial could be nothing but a farce. Izko was condemned to death although there was no evidence against him. The tribunal was a military one, although many of the 'accused' had already been condemned for the same or similar actions by a civil court. The judges were army officers ignorant of the law, except for one who had enough juridical knowledge to advise the soldiers. The lawyers were constantly threatened with imprisonment by the president of the tribunal, and had difficulty in expressing themselves.

The accused, chained together, were calm and haughty. They fought continually, not to defend themselves against the accusations of their oppressors, but to proclaim, in the hearing of the press, the tortures to which they had been subjected, to which the president, seeing that he could not silence them, replied, inevitably, 'Irrelevant'. It was clear to the reporters that these soldiers had been mustered not to judge but to kill. They went conscientiously through an absurd ceremony with which they were unfamiliar. 'The accused' laid bare the oppressive violence of 'Spain'. They forbade the lawyers to defend them. They won. Their admirable courage and the obtuse idiocy of the judges made the trial the concern of all Basques. When the workers of the big concerns in Bilbao went on strike ETA knew that it had involved large sections of the working class.

Besides indignation was so widespread throughout the world that for the first time the Basque question stood before international opinion. Euskadi became known everywhere as a martyred nation, fighting for its independence. The reaction of general anger recoiled on the government. The death penalties were commuted. ETA by this un-asked-for but necessary victory for its tactics was publicly confirmed as the spearhead of the working class. The entire nation was mobilized and ETA acquired considerable prestige, as PNV had done twenty-five years previously. The militants know that there is a long struggle ahead, that it could take twenty or thirty years to build up a people's army. No matter. In Burgos, between December 1970 and January 1971, the challenge had been thrown down.

So here we are, we French, who willy-nilly, are always somewhat the heirs of Jacobinism! A heroic people, led by a revolutionary party, has given us a glimpse of the 'other' socialism, decentralist and concrete, the singular universality that ETA rightly sets up in opposition to the abstract centralism of its oppressors. Is this socialism viable for all? Isn't it only a provisional solution for colonised countries? In other terms, can we foresee that this is the end of a stage towards the time when universal exploitation will come to an end and all men will enjoy equally a true universalism by the common operation of all particularisms? This is a problem for the colonialists. We can be sure that the colonials, fighting for independence, have no problem.

What is certain in the eyes of the Basque militants is that the right of people to self determination, affirmed in the most radical necessity, implies everywhere the revision of all present frontiers, which are the residue of bourgeois expansion, corresponding nowhere to the needs of peoples. And this can only be achieved by a cultural revolution, which will create a socialist man, on the foundations of his land, his language and his renovated customs. It is from this point alone that man will gradually cease to be the product of his product and will at the last become the son of man. Can we concur in these marxist conceptions? We may note at this point some doubts among the ETA leaders. Some call themselves neo-marxists, and others apparently the majority, 'marxist-leninists'. The day to day realities of the struggle will decide. As Ché Guevara once said to me, 'Are we Marxists? I don't know' adding with a smile, 'it's not our fault if reality is Marxist'. What ETA has shown us is the need of all men to affirm (including the centralists) their particularisms against abstract universalism. For us to listen to the Basques, the Bretons and the Occitans, to fight at their side so that they may affirm their concrete singularity, is, as a direct consequence, to fight for ourselves as French people, for the true independence of France, which is the first victim of its own centralism. For there exists a Basque people and a Breton people, but Jacobinism and industrialisation have liquidated our people, today there are only French masses.

Appendix B
The Scottish Nationalist manifesto

It's Time: October 10 presents the people of Scotland with an historic opportunity. The decision we make will determine whether we are to enjoy prosperity as citizens of a democratic, self-governing country, or declining living standards in an exploited province of the United Kingdom.

A vote for either the Conservative Party or the Labour Party will be a vote for a party that has failed Scotland consistently for fifty years. A vote for the SNP will be a vote of confidence in your own ability to make Scotland a socially just and prosperous community.

The Scottish National Party is the fastest-growing political party in Europe. It has doubled its vote at every election since 1959 and it is the party that gets results. The 632,032 votes it won last February produced seven MPs and a flood of concessions to Scotland from the London political parties. Even more important for the future of Scotland those votes put the issue of self-government for Scotland at the centre of Scottish politics. As a result the alternatives for Scottish voters are clearer than ever before.

Today the United Kingdom faces its most serious economic crisis since the Second World War. A record balance of payments deficit, record inflation and the prospect of record levels of post-war unemployment are combining to threaten the average family with a falling standard of living for the first time since immediately after the war.

The crisis does not come as a bolt from the blue. The action of the Arab oil states in raising the price of the imported oil on which the United Kingdom's economy depends may have brought the day of reckoning forward. But the United

Kingdom's economic record before last October's rise in the price of oil was a succession of economic crises, each more serious than the one before.

Successive governments have run through a long list of attempted solutions. Devaluation, cuts in overseas defence commitments, voluntary incomes policies, national economic plans and the councils to execute them, statutory prices and incomes policies with the boards to administer them, social contracts and compacts, industrial relations legislation, floating the pound and all kinds of freezes and squeezes and stop-go policies . . . They have all been tried and they have failed – without exception.

Finally, Mr Heath's Conservative Government, continuing the policy of its Labour predecessor, took the United Kingdom into the Common Market in 1973, against the votes of a majority of Scotland's MPs and the wishes of a majority of the Scottish people. It was an act of political desperation and the people of Scotland, along with the people of England and Wales, are suffering the consequences in food shortages, price rises and industrial decline.

Scotland has paid a bitter price for the United Kingdom's record of economic failure. Unemployment has been between one and a half times to twice the United Kingdom average. Household incomes have been more than £5 lower in Scotland than in south-east England and prices five per cent higher than the United Kingdom average. One in five of Scotland's population has to endure a standard of living on, or close to, the official "poverty line". Scotland's housing is the worst in western Europe with 220,000 houses officially classified as sub-standard. Infant mortality rates and adult sickness rates are higher and life expectancy lower.

The record is summed up in a recent report by the National Children's Bureau, *Born to Fail?* which concludes that where one in 47 children in south-east England is "socially disadvantaged", in Scotland the proportion is one in 10.

The current economic crisis in the United Kingdom contains new dangers for Scotland. Unemployment, already approaching the 100,000 mark, is likely within 18 months to rise well beyond it to levels unknown since the depression of the 1930s. Twenty per cent inflation is cutting into the living standards of all sections of the community and hitting hardest at the economically weak. And in spite of all the big promises by Tory and Labour politicians no London government, faced with economic crisis on the present scale, will have the money or credit to carry through the economic and social reconstruction which Scotland so desperately needs.

But the crisis in the United Kingdom is not just economic. Persistent economic failure and Punch and Judy politicking has destroyed the authority and prestige of London politicians. The public is sick of the diet of unfulfilled promises, of "jam tomorrow", which it has been fed by the Labour and Tory parties. As the crisis deepens, extremism in England threatens to swamp commonsense and destroy constructive political debate. The value of democracy itself is being questioned. London has lost confidence in its ability to master events. There is a hint of Weimar in the English autumn.

A vote for Tory or Labour is a vote for continuing to be part of a demoralized state whose politicians cannot find the answers to the familiar problems of their own country, England, let alone make good the promies of reforms they are now lavishing on Scotland.

Full self-government: The prospects for a self-governing Scotland stand in clear contrast. Scotland's population, unlike that of England, is in reasonable balance with her natural resources. In a world of growing shortages Scotland is richly provided with many of the basic elements of wealth.

We are self-sufficient, in trading terms, in agricultural products. We have abundant resources of water and of space for economic development and for recreation. We have plentiful fishing stocks, if properly conserved. With appropriate investment we could be self-sufficient in timber and its products.

Scotland's industrial sector, although weakened in some aspects by the neglect of remote government and in others by inadequate investment, produces a wide variety of manufactured goods in high demand in the markets of the world. And in the crucial field of energy, Scotland with her reserves of coal gas and oil, as well as her expertise in nuclear generation can be compared only with Norway, among

177

European nations.

Even the opponents of self-government now admit that these resources, if developed under Scottish control for the benefit of the people of Scotland, could put Scotland alongside Norway, Sweden and Switzerland as one of the most prosperous countries in the world.

It's Scotland's oil: Scotland's oil provides the most vivid illustration of how much there is to gain and how much to lose on October 10.

London governments whether Labour or Tory or a coalition of English parties, need to exploit Scotland's oil with the greatest possible speed in order to reduce the United Kingdom's balance of payments deficit. But the London smash and grab of Scotland's oil is causing the maximum of social and environmental damage while bringing the minimum of economic benefit. Scottish industry is not being given time to equip itself to take advantage of the industrial opportunities. The jobs generated by the construction boom will be short-lived leaving Scotland's unemployment problems as bad after the oil had been exhausted as before its discovery.

Oil: At the rate of extraction necessary to achieve London's target of self-sufficiency in oil by 1980 Scotland's output of oil will be in decline within 10 years and revenues from the oil will have to be used to pay the interest on the massive loans the London government has already started to raise abroad to cover the accumulated deficit on the balance of payments. Nothing will be left to pay for the economic and social reconstruction of Scotland.

A Scottish government, by contrast, would control the oil companies' operation to ensure the development of the oil at a rate which suits Scotland's interests not those of London, the Common Market, or the United States. A production rate of 50m tons annually would meet Scotland's own need for oil – some 12m tons per year – while leaving a generous surplus for export to England and elsewhere. Scottish firms would have time to establish a stake in the oil industry thereby providing secure long-term employment. Stringent conditions would be laid down to safeguard Scotland's natural environment. A rash of "boom and bust" construction yards would be avoided. The reserves would last for several generations instead of being exhausted within a single generation, and the annual revenues of more than £1,000m would be used to build the houses, schools and hospitals we need to create sufficient long-term jobs in modern industries to reduce Scotland's unemployment to the Norwegian level of less than one per cent, to pay for higher pensions and benefits for the sick, the disabled and the dependent and to give aid to the countries of the third world.

Self-government – the issues: Self-government is a matter of principle; but it also provides the only effective way of dealing with the practical problems that are facing the people of Scotland.

Prices: A self-governing Scotland would be in a strong position to control the rate of price rises.

1. The Scottish pound supported by Scotland's balance of payments surplus could maintain its purchasing power abroad unlike the pound sterling which fell in value by 46 per cent last year against major commodities.

2. The Scottish pound, unlike sterling, would not need to be supported by borrowing at exorbitant rates of interest which push up costs throughout industry and public sector.

3. The development with self-government of Scotland's great economic potential would ensure that demands for higher and more secure living standards could be met out of increases in *real* wealth, not as at present in the United Kingdom out of increases in counterfeit wealth created by printing more money. As a result the value of the pound – the *Scottish* pound in your pocket – would be maintained.

4. These advantages would free wage and salary earners from the chronic insecurity which, within the United Kingdom, impels them to demand wage and salary increases in anticipation of continued increases in the rate of price rises, so fuelling the upward spiral of inflation.

5. Against such a background of economic confidence the statutory wage freezes to which successive London governments have been driven as measures of last resorts would be unnecessary and indeed harmful to the spirit of co-operation needed to rebuild Scotland.

In the short term the SNP proposes a price freeze on essential foodstuffs with the existing machinery of the Prices

Commission used to provide selective subsidies to producers and suppliers faced with increased costs which they cannot absorb.

Jobs: It is expected that over the next seven years 500,000 additional jobs will be needed in Scotland to eliminate existing unemployment, cater for returning emigrants, replace jobs likely to disappear (including many which are scarcely worth having at present) and allow for an increase in activity rates.

The Scottish National Party proposes the establishment of an industrial development corporation financed, in part, by oil revenues and able to attract investment capital from private sources, to be charged with stimulating and, if appropriate, undertaking on its own behalf investment in new technologically advanced industries offering secure long-term employment throughout Scotland. It would be supported by a network of regional offices enjoying wide powers of discretion and would provide venture capital for new entrepreneurial talents, especially for projects based on principles of industrial democracy and co-operation.

Tens of thousands of Scottish jobs will be lost in the next two years as the economic crisis deepens in the United Kingdom. The Scottish National Party believes that the unemployment crisis makes more urgent than ever the swift establishment of an effective Scottish parliament with powers over trade and industry, including the powers to establish and finance an industrial development corporation as described.

Food: In a world of growing shortages the full development of Scotland's food producing potential deserves the highest priority. The confidence of Scotland's farmers has been destroyed by the combined effects of the previous Government's determination to take the United Kingdom into the Common Market and the present Government's failure to prepare for any of the problems of adapting to the new system of agricultural support. Today's farming crisis is tomorrow's food shortage: the farmers must be given security by the emergency reintroduction of a deficiency payments system and in the longer term by the introduction of a price review based on a five or seven-year plan.

Fishing limits will be extended, with international

agreement, to the extent necessary to safeguard Scottish fishing stocks.

Housing: Rents in both the public and private sector will be frozen until a more just system of housing finance can be implemented. Currently the main pressure for rent increases comes from rising interest rates and the high cost of building land. SNP policy will aim to contain and reduce these costs.

A major programme of house-building will be launched with the aim of eliminating sub-standard housing and homelessness within seven years.

Notes

Chapter One

[1] 'What's Happening?' in Occitan.
[2] *Time,* September 3rd, 1973.
[3] *Newsweek,* August 12th, 1974.
[4] Roger McGough, *Observer,* July 21st, 1974, back page.
[5] Ann Sheehy, *The Crimean Tatars* (Minority Rights Group, report no. 6).
[6] *The Sovereign State of I.T.T.,* (Hodder & Stoughton, London, 1973).
[7] Quoted in Jean-Jacques Servan-Schreiber, *Le Pouvoir Régional* (Grasset, Paris, 1971), pp. 49-50.
[8] Grasset, Paris, 1971
[9] *Le Point,* August 27th, 1973.

Chapter Two

[1] 'Long Live the Basques' in Basque.
[2] *Encyclopaedia Britannica.*
[3] Hugh Thomas, *The Spanish Civil War* (Eyre & Spottiswoode, London, 1961).
[4] Santiago Carrillo, Director of the Spanish Communist Party, in exile.

Chapter Three

[1] 'No Smoking' in Welsh.
[2] Blond and Briggs, London, 1973.
[3] Reprinted in *Planet* magazine, February/March, 1971.
[4] *Western Mail,* November 30th, 1973.

Chapter Four

1. 'Where are we going?' in Romani.
2. Kenrick and Puxon, *The Destiny of Europe's Gypsies* (Heinemann, London, 1972).
3. Ibid
4. Gratton Puxon, *The Rom: The Gypsies of Europe* (Minority Rights Group, report no. 14).
5. August/September 1973, Paris.
6. Puxon, op. cit.
7. Ibid.
8. Ibid.
9. Ibid.
10. Ibid.

Chapter Five

1. 'Long Live Brittany' in Breton.
2. Following Celtic History based on series of articles by Martyn Rhys Vaughn in *Welsh Nation* (official newspaper of Plaid Cymru).
3. Morvan Lebesque, *Comment Peut-on Etre Breton?* (Editions Seuil, Paris, 1970).

Chapter Six

1. 'Mohawk' in Mohawk.

Chapter Seven

1. 'Waiting for Godot', in Catalan.
2. George Orwell, *Homage to Catalonia* (Secker & Warburg, London, 1938).
3. Quoted in *The Spanish Civil War* by Hugh Thomas (Eyre & Spottiswoode, London, 1961).
4. Catalan is, however, the official language of the tiny semi-autonomous Pyrenean republic of Andorra.

Chapter Eight

1. 'Lapp' in Lappish (rhymes with sauna).
2. In *The Lapps in Sweden* by Israel Ruong (Swedish Institute, Stockholm, 1967).

[3] Jonathan Cape, London, 1967.

Chapter Nine
[1] October 1974.

Appendix A
[1] Translation in *Planet* Magazine, no. 9, December 1971.

Bibliography

Barth, Fredrik (ed.), *Ethnic Groups and Boundaries* (Allen and Unwin, London, 1969)

Bonjour, E., H. S. Offler and G. R. Potter, *A Short History of Switzerland* (Oxford University Press, London, 1955)

Bouffanet, Bernard (text), plus misc. photographers, *Le Larzac Veut Vivre* (Daniel Mauprey, Paris, 1973)

Brown, Dee, *Bury My Heart at Wounded Knee* (Barry and Jenkins, London, 1971)

Carter, Vincent O., *The Bern Book* (Macmillan, London, 1973)

Chadwick, Nora, *The Celts* (Pelican, Harmondsworth, 1970)

Clébert, Jean-Paul, *The Gypsies* (Vista Books, London, 1963)

Cobham, Alfred, *The Nation State and National Self-Determination* (Fontana, London, 1969)

Ecologist, A Blueprint for Survival (Penguin, Harmondsworth, 1973)

Economic Plan for Wales (Plaid Cymru Research Group, Cardiff, 1970)

Eidheim, Harald, *Aspects of the Lappish Minority Situation* (Scandinavian University Books, Oslo, 1971)

Evans, Gwynfor, *Wales Can Win* (Christopher Davies, Carmarthenshire, 1973)

FLB 72/ Procès de la Bretagne (Editions Kelenn, France, 1973)

Friendly, Alfred, *Israel's Oriental Immigrants and Druzes* (Minority Rights Group, report no. 12)

Héraud, Guy, *Peuples et Langues d'Europe* (Denoël, Paris, 1966)

Héraud, Guy, and Roland Béguelin, *Europe-Jura* (Rassemblement Jurassien, Delemont, Switzerland, 1965)

Huber, Hans, *How Switzerland is Governed* (Schweizer Spiegel, Zurich, 1968)

Isaba, Patxi, *Euzkadi Socialiste* (Editions du Cercle, Paris, 1971)

Jackson, Harold, *The Two Irelands* (Minority Rights Group, report no. 2)

Jackson, W. Eric, *Local Government in England and Wales* (Pelican, Harmondsworth, 1971)

Jaulin, Robert, *La Paix Blanche* (Editions Seuil, Paris, 1970)

Jones, R. M., *Highlights in Welsh Literature* (Christopher Davies, Carmarthenshire, 1969)

Kenrick, Donald, and Gratton Puxon, *The Destiny of Europe's Gypsies* (Heinemann, London, 1972)

Kohr, Leopold, *Development Without Aid* (Christopher Davies, Carmarthenshire, 1974)

Lafont, Robert, *Clefs Pour L'Occitainie* (Editions Seghers, Paris, 1971)

Lafont, Robert (ed.), *Le Sud et Le Nord* (Edouard Privat, Paris, 1971)

The Lapps Today, I and II (The Nordic Lapp Council, Mouton, Paris)

Le Bris, Michel, *Occitanie: Volem Viure* (Gallimard, Paris, 1974)

Lebesque, Morvan, *Comment Peut-on Etre Breton?* (Editions Seuil, Paris, 1970)

Les Temps Modernes, August/September 1973: 'Minorités Nationales en France' (Paris)

Luethy, Herbert, *France Against Herself* (Meridian Books, New York, 1959)

Medhurst, Kenneth, *The Basques* (Minority Rights Group, report no. 9)

Puxon, Gratton, *The Rom: The Gypsies of Europe* (Minority Rights Group, report no. 14)

Ruong, Israel, *The Lapps in Sweden* (Swedish Institute, Stockholm, 1967)

Sampson, Anthony, *The New Europeans* (Hodder and Stoughton, London 1962)

Sampson, Anthony, *The Sovereign State of I.T.T.* (Hodder and Stoughton, London, 1973)

Schumacher, E. F., *Small is Beautiful* (Blond and Briggs, London, 1973)

Serant, Paul, *La France des Minorités* (Robert Laffont, Paris,

1965)

Servan-Schreiber, Jean-Jaques, *Le Pouvoir Régional* (Grasset, Paris, 1971)

Sheehy, Ann, *The Crimean Tatars, Volga Germans and Meshkhetians* (Minority Rights Group, report no. 6)

Taylor, A. J. P., *Europe: Grandeur and Decline*, 3 vols (Hamish Hamilton, London, 1950–56)

Thomas, Hugh, *The Spanish Civil War* (Eyre and Spottiswoode, London, 1961)

Thomas, Ned, *The Welsh Extremist* (Y Lolfa, Caredigion, Wales, 1973)

Whetter, Dr James, *A Celtic Tomorrow: Essays in Cornish Nationalism* (M. K. Publications, St Austell, 1973)

Wilson, Edmund, *Apolgies to the Iroquois* (W. H. Allen, London, 1960)

Useful Addresses

Basque

Euskal Elkargoa (in French) Newsletter
16 rue de la République
64500-St-Jean-de Luz
France

Basque Government in Exile
48 rue Singer
Paris 16
France

Brittany

Douar Breiz (Mlle Kerhuel's newsletter, in French)
22530-Mur-de-Bretagne
France

Parti Communiste Breton (publish newspaper)
8 rue d'Argentré
35000 Rennes
France

Catalonia

Omnium Culturel
Palau Delmases
Montcada 20
Barcelona 3
Spain

Encyclopedia Catalana
Via Layetana, 171
Barcelona
Spain

Gypsies

World Romani Congress
Residence les Fougères
Batiment D5
Avon-77210
France

Gypsy Council
c/o Minority Rights Group
Benjamin Franklin House
36 Craven Street
London WC2
England

Lapps

Sámi Institut'ta (Lapp Institute)
Kautokeino
Norway

Occitania

Lutte Occitane
BP 2138
34026-Montpelier-Cedex
France

P.N.O.
1 rue Albert André
30 Bagnols
France

Mohawk

Akwesasne Notes
Mohawk Nation via Rooseveltown
New York 13683
U.S.A.

Wales

Plaid Cymru
8 Queen Street
Cardiff
Wales

Welsh Nation (weekly newspaper of Plaid Cymru)
8 Queen Street
Cardiff
Wales

Planet (quarterly magazine in English)
Llangeitho
Tregaron
Cardiganshire
Wales

Welsh Language Society
24 Fford y Môr
Aberystwyth
Wales

Switzerland

Tout Va Bien (Marxist magazine in French)
Case Postal 87
1213 Petit-Lancy-1
Switzerland

Rassemblement Jurassien (Jurassien Liberation Front)
Delémont
Jura
Switzerland

Cornwall

Cornish Banner (organ of the Cornish Nationalist Party)
Trelispen
Gorran
St Austell
Cornwall